First Certificate

Practice

Tests ▶ Plus

N Kenny
L Luque-Mortimer

Longman

Pearson Education Limited
Edinburgh Gate
Harlow
Essex CM20 2JE
England
And Associated Companies throughout the World

www.longman-elt.com

ISBN 0 582 40579 3

Set in 10pt Frutiger Light

Printed in Spain by Graficas Estella

Acknowledgements

We are grateful to the following for permission to reproduce copyright photographs:

All Action/Justin Thomas for 156 bottom; BBC Photograph Library for 165 bottom right; Britstock-IFA for 166 bottom; Bubbles Photo Library/Pauline Cutler for 152 bottom; Format/Jacky Chapman for 156 middle right; Robert Harding Picture Library for 154 top, 154 bottom, 158 top, 158 bottom, 161 top, 161 bottom, 163 top, 163 bottom, 167 top, 168 bottom left, 168 bottom right, 169 top, 170 bottom, 173 top and 173 bottom; Image Bank for 155 bottom, 164 left, 168 top right, 170 top and 172 bottom; Images Colour Library for 156 middle left, 160 bottom, 164 right, 165 middle right, 168 middle left, 174 top right, 174 middle left, 174 top right and 174 bottom right; Photo Edit for 162 middle left; Powerstock Zefa for 155 top; Redferns/Leon Morris for 162 middle right; Retna/Jenny Acheson for 152 top; Science Photo Library/David Ducros for 162 bottom; St. Edmunds College, Ware/Les Warr for 151 top; Stay Still/Mark Harris for 151 bottom; The Stock Market for 167 bottom; Tony Stone Images for 162 top left, 165 top right and 174 bottom left; Telegraph Colour Library for 156 top left (VCL), 156 top right (FPG/Stephen Simpson), 157 top (Masterfile), 157 bottom (Masterfile), 160 top (Michael Dunning), 165 top left (Philippe Poulet/Mission), 165 bottom left (Masterfile), 166 top (Paul Campbell), 168 top left (Jeff Sherman), 169 bottom (Masterfile) and 173 top (King Shipman Production) and Topham Picturepoint/Press Association for 162 top right.

We are grateful to the following for permission to reproduce copyright material:

Albedo One for an adapted extract from the article 'Interview with Terry Brooks' by Robert Neilson in ALBEDO ONE Issue Winter 1997/8; BA Education for an extract adapted from an article on collecting Teddy Bears by Brian Allensby on www.ba-education.demon.co.uk/break/col/teddy.html; BBC Wildlife Magazine for an adapted extract from the article 'How to be animal friendly' in BBC WILDLIFE magazine 9.99; BBC Magazines for an adapted extract from the article 'Singing: ticket to a musical life' by Roderic Dunnet in BBC MUSIC magazine Nov 1994;

Diver Magazine UK for an adapted extract from the article 'True Stories – Interviews with Diving Instrustors' in DIVER; authors' agents Curtis Brown Limited on behalf of the Estate of Gerald Durrell for an adapted extract from MENAGERIE MANOR published by HarperCollins; Elle (UK) for an adapted extract from the article 'London, Paris, Milan, Uganda' by Iain Webb in ELLE March 1999; Express Newspapers for adapted extracts from the article 'Voice in a million' by Sally Staples in SUNDAY EXPRESS CLASSIC 14.1.96, 'Golfball Frogman' by Roger Collier in EXPRESS ON SUNDAY Magazine 9.11.97 and 'The queen of urban chic' by Michelle Stanistreet in SUNDAY EXPRESS SMART MONEY 19.9.99, © Express Newspapers; Geographical Magazine for adapted extracts from the articles 'More than a rock show' by Fiona McWilliam in GEOGRAPHICAL magazine 7/96 and 'Fighting fit' by Sophie Cooke in GEOGRAPHICAL magazine 11/99; Graphters Ltd for an adapted extract from the article 'Whales' by Hilary Champion in EUROPEAN LIFE Summer 1999; Guardian News Service Limited for adapted extracts from the articles 'Huge Steps of Going Round' by Alex Bellos in THE GUARDIAN 27.3.99, 'Staying Power' by Karen Williams in THE GUARDIAN 13.4.99, 'It's up, up and away' by Eileen Sheridan in THE GUARDIAN 29.5.99, 'Jobs in animation are a real draw' by Philip Inman from 'Up Front' in THE GUARDIAN 19.6.99, 'Fast Track Studies' by Oliver Swanton in THE GUARDIAN 3.8.99, 'Blackpool's novel idea' by Jerome Monahan in GUARDIAN EDUCATION 10.8.99, 'Little big man' in THE GUARDIAN WEEKEND REVIEW 31.7.99, 'Everything is grand in the parlour as the piano turns fashion forte' by Neasa MacErlean in THE OBSERVER (Cash Section) 15.8.99, 'Bulletin' by Ursula Kenny in THE OBSERVER magazine 8.8.99 and 'Going solo – with the flying aunties' by Majorie Yue in OBSERVER ESCAPE 15.8.99; Robert Harding Syndication for adapted extracts from the articles 'A head for figures' by Melanie Jones in INSPIRATIONS June 1996 and 'Making Mirrors' by Helen Chislett in INSPIRATIONS Sept 1999; Haynes Publishing for an adapted extract from BICYCLES UP KILIMANJARO by Nicholas and Richard Crane published in 1988 by Oxford Illustrated Press, an imprint of Haynes Publishing; Illustrated London News for an adapted extract from the article 'Amuse' by Charles Campion in THE ILLUSTRATED LONDON NEWS Summer 1998; Independent Newspapers UK Ltd for adapted extracts from the articles 'Having second thoughts' by Lola Brown and 'Ideal Homes?' by Katherine Lea in YOU CAN! supplement published in association with THE INDEPENDENT April 1999; IPC Magazines for an extract by Camilla Bonn form COUNTRY LIFE MAGAZINE 12.2.98 © Camilla Brown/Country Life 1998; the author, Dylan Jones for an extract adapted from his article 'Mister' in THE INDEPENDENT Magazine 18.1.97 (Dylan Jones is editor of GQ magazine); National Geographic for adapted extracts from the articles 'Learning to live with mountain lions' by Maurice G Hornocker in NATIONAL GEOGRAPHIC July 1992 and 'On Assignment' in NATIONAL GEOGRAPHIC 12/92, 7/92, 7/93 and 1/94; The National Magazine Company for adapted extracts from the articles 'Does your man need a makeover?' by Gilly Turney in GOOD HOUSEKEEPING October 1998 and 'I just had to write' by Gillian Fairchild in GOOD HOUSEKEEPING November 1998, © National Magazine Company; National World Magazine for an adapted extract form the article 'Trees for life' by Chris Barnes in NATURAL WORLD magazine Spring/Summer 1996; News Syndication Limited for adapted extracts from the articles 'Young, hip and dangerous' by Jennai Cox in 'This life' supplement Part 6 in THE TIMES 24.10.98, 'Send in the Clowns' by John Naish in 'This Life' Supplement in THE TIMES 24.10.98 © Times Newspapers Limited 1998, 'I'm ready to face the ocean of dreams' by Jonathan Gornall in THE TIMES 21.8.99 © Times Newspapers Limited 21.8.99, 'Waste not want not, produces a tasty recipe that sells soup' by Veronica Heath in THE TIMES 3.11.98 © Veronica Heath/Times Newspapers Limited 3.11.89 and 'Liquorice Oldsorts' by Paul Crosbie in THE SUN 9.7.99 © News International Newspapers Limited 1999; The Oban Times for an extract from the article 'Shadows along the shore' by Keith Broomfield in SCOTTISH FIELD magazine August 1999; Oxford University Press for an adapted extract from 'Penguins' in THE LIVING WORLD 1993; Solo Syndication for adapted extracts from the articles 'The good buy man' by Nicole Swengley in THE EVENING STANDARD 24.6.99, 'Professional Secretary' by Kate Crockett in EVENING STANDARD 19.7.99, 'The life of Ryan' by Sheila Johnston in HOT TICKETS MAGAZINE/EVENING STANDARD July 1999, 'A day in the life of an archaeologist' by Ben West in HOT TICKETS MAGAZINE/EVENING STANDARD 19.7.99 and 'Wild Ryder' by Sheila Johnston in HOT TICKETS MAGAZINE/EVENING STANDARD 5.8.99; Space Future for an adapted extract from the website http//spacefuture.com/tourism/gettingthere.html; Telegraph Newspapers Limited for an adapted extract from the article 'Waveboarding' by Phil Young in DAILY TELEGRAPH 26.6.99 and the author, Nigel Tisdall for an adapted extract from his article 'All I had to protect me was a leaflet' in SUNDAY TELEGRAPH TRAVEL 16.5.99.

We have been unable to trace the copyright holders of the articles 'Signs of Life' by Paul Morrison, 'Britain's wildest place' by Jon Orchard, 'Across to Puffin Island' by Andrew Osmond, 'Tricks of the trade: Virgin trekking' by Graham Thompson and 'Put my TV down it's Friends!' by Amanda Volley and would appreciate any information that would enable us to do so.

Designed by Michael Harris
Project managed by Jayne Wildman
Illustrations by Joan Corlass

Contents

TEST 1

Reading (1 hour 15 minutes)

You are going to read an article about hot air balloons. Choose the most suitable heading from the list **A–I** for each part (**1–7**) of the article. There is one extra heading which you do not need to use. There is an example at the beginning (**0**).

Mark your answers **on the separate answer sheet**.

A	Involving balloon passengers
B	Qualifying as a balloon flyer
C	The price of balloons
D	Balloons for special occasions
E	The joy of achievement
F	Restrictions on passengers
G	Flying your balloon: practical considerations
H	The superiority of balloons
I	The inventors' expectations

Tip Strip

- Read the text quickly for general understanding.
- You only need to understand the main point of each paragraph. Don't worry if you don't understand every word.
- Read each paragraph, decide what the main point is, then find the best heading. Be careful – the headings won't use the same words as the text.
- When you have read all the paragraphs, go back and check your answers.

Paragraph 3: This refers to rules and limitations. Can you find a similar phrase in the headings?

Paragraph 7: Who is this advice for?

Heading A: What does 'involving' mean? Participate?

Heading B: 'Qualifying' suggests you need to take exams. Which paragraph mentions this?

Heading H: This heading suggests comparison. In which paragraph are balloons compared to other means of transport?

It's up, up and away

Eileen Shaw on the joys of ballooning

---

0 | *I*

Mostly it's about hot air – for without that, balloons are just big empty bags with baskets on the bottom. The Montgolfier brothers had great hopes when they made the first manned flight. They thought balloons would take off as a viable means of commercial flight. Instead, they have remained the province of sport, adventure and enjoyment.

1

Modern balloons are a lot more sophisticated than their ancestors, but they still retain the essential characteristics which makes them so attractive. A plane is claustrophobic and very noisy. Balloons are so gentle and majestic and silent when the burner's not working. 'It's the most marvellous form of aviation,' says Chris Boyd, managing director of *Hot Air Balloons*.

2

Hot Air Balloons offers balloon trips suited to the requirements of customers, with unlimited possibilities. Celebrations are high on the list of reasons for booking a balloon flight. 'Birthdays, anniversaries, we even had a couple who wanted to get married during the flight, but we told them that wouldn't be allowed,' says Chris.

3

He takes parties of four to twelve, the maximum number allowed, and there is no age limit at the upper end – he has had a 92-year-old customer. The only other rule is that you have to be at least one metre tall, so small children are not allowed on board. This is because the side of the baskets is adult chest height and youngsters might be tempted to climb up to look out.

4

An ordinary flight lasts about an hour and a half and can reach over 1,000 metres. The cost of a flight covers four hours and includes a certificate for first-time flyers. The important point is that you don't just turn up and climb on board. You are invited to take an active part, so before the flight you spend about 45 minutes helping to inflate the balloon and getting to know it.

5

At the end of the trip, passengers are served with champagne and nibbles. Champagne is traditional after balloon flights. 'Most people are very happy that they have done it because they might have been a bit anxious before they set out, so they are glad to celebrate the experience,' he says.

6

So, taking a trip is one pleasure, but what if you fancy owning your own balloon? First, you will need a balloon licence. To get a licence you can train with a company like *Hot Air Balloons* and do 16 hours' flying with an instructor. Then you have to take written exams in the technical aspects of the balloon and other subjects.

7

When you own a balloon, you will need a trailer to store it and tow it to the launch site and someone to follow you to pick you up when you land. You may need a landowner's permission to start your flight, but it is possible to start from a very large garden. You can read all about how to get started in a new quarterly magazine for balloon enthusiasts published by the Balloon and Airship Club.

You are going to read a newspaper article about the sport of inline skating. For Questions **8–15**, choose the correct answer **A**, **B**, **C** or **D**.

Mark your answers **on the separate answer sheet**.

Inline Skating

Tracy Winters is on a mission to change the image of inline skating in this country

In her skates there is no stopping Tracy Winters. She spends most of her time teaching, consulting, examining or campaigning on behalf of this country's ever-growing number of inline skaters.

Busy as she is, Tracy did manage to spare an hour early one Saturday morning to give me a lesson in the local park. The slight unease I felt at never having used inline skates before was not helped, however, by her emphatic disapproval as I pulled a pair of brand-new skates from my bag.

'Oh dear,' she said with a frown. 'You've been sold what we call 'aggressive' skates, which are no good for the sort of skating that you want to do. They're too heavy for twists and turns and the wheels are too small. And you've no brake.'

'But I was told that all I need to do to stop was drag my leg behind me,' I protested.

'No, no, no,' said Tracy. She explained how she was currently helping a girl who has been off work for a year with a damaged leg after following similar advice. Tracy is drawing up a list of guidelines for selling inline skates based on ability, budget and type of use, which she wants to see all retailers use. She has seen the purchase of inappropriate skates all too often before. 'What you should have been sold is recreational skates,' she told me.

Ordinarily, those who turn up with the wrong skates suffer the added annoyance of missing out on a lesson because Tracy will not teach them. I was more fortunate and, after a small **ticking off** for not having knee pads, my lesson began.

Away from the critical eyes of more experienced skaters, she started me off gently, simple skating up and down a track on the edge of the park.

'Hands out,' Tracy told me repeatedly. **This** was not just to help break a fall, but to prevent my tumbling altogether. Ice skaters, Tracy pointed out, keep their arms in front not only to look elegant: it actually keeps them balanced.

To help get rid of my fear, Tracy insisted that a fall would be good for me, but that I would need to relax for this to reduce the chances of injury. I was not so keen, but obeyed each time she reminded me to keep my back straight and chin up. 'You don't look at the ground when you're riding a bike,' she said.

Apart from ice-skating and bicycle riding, inline skating has similarities with ballet and skiing, which makes it attractive to a wide range of people. An estimated sixty percent of inline skate owners use them every week and more than half are recreational skaters. In this country the sport is regarded as something for the young and as potentially dangerous. Tracy, together with the National Inline Skating Association, is trying to change this impression, in the first instance by emphasising the importance of insurance and the wearing of protective clothing in case of accidents. She would also like to see the sport more widely catered for in sports centres and health clubs, possibly through the building of indoor skating arenas.

Having been on wheels almost every day of her life since the age of five, Tracy is well-versed in the virtues of skating and, she claims, she never tires of the sport. 'It is the feeling of moving, of gliding, I can't quite pin it down, but it makes me feel good,' she says. Like the hundreds who start skating every week, I now know what she means.

8 How did the writer feel before her inline skating lesson?

   A a little nervous
   B quite confident
   C very frightened
   D extremely excited

9 What was wrong with the skates which the writer bought?

   A They were of poor quality.
   B They were not suitable.
   C They did not fit her well.
   D They didn't work properly.

10 Why is Tracy writing a set of guidelines?

   A to help people who have been injured
   B to advise people who are buying skates
   C to provide information to sales staff in shops
   D to tell her students what to bring to lessons

11 'ticking off' in line 32 means

   A checking something.
   B waiting for something.
   C giving someone a reward.
   D telling someone they're wrong.

12 What does 'this' in line 37 refer to?

   A simple skating
   B repeated instructions
   C use of the hands
   D avoiding falls

13 Tracy compares skating and cycling in terms of

   A the fear people feel at first.
   B the need to learn how to fall.
   C the need to relax to keep balanced.
   D the correct body position to adopt.

14 How would Tracy like to change the idea people have of inline skating?

   A by encouraging older people to do it
   B by discouraging recreational skating
   C by stressing the need for safety
   D by forming a national association

15 After the lesson, the writer agrees with Tracy that inline skating

   A is easy to learn.
   B is rather tiring.
   C is hard to teach.
   D is very satisfying.

Tip Strip

- The questions follow the order of the text.
- Read the text carefully. Don't worry if you don't understand every word.
- Try to answer the question, or complete the sentence, before you look at options A, B, C and D.
- Underline key words in the question, e.g. 'How did the writer feel before ...' then find the part of the text where the answer is and underline words there, e.g. the slight unease I felt.
- Find the option which best matches the text, e.g. in paragraph 2 'slight' means 'not much' and 'unease' is a negative emotion, so the right answer is 8A.

Question 10: Be careful! Tracy mentions 'retailers', which is another word for ... ?

Question 11: What type of person is Tracy? Does she think the writer is well-prepared for the lesson?

Question 12: Does 'this' refer to something earlier or later in the text?

Question 13: When does Tracy mention cycling? Why?

Question 14: What idea *do* people have of the sport? What does Tracy think about this?

You are going to read a magazine article about the Hebrides Islands in Scotland. Seven sentences have been removed from the article. Choose from the sentences **A–H** the one which fits each gap (**16–21**). There is one extra sentence which you do not need to use. There is an example at the beginning (**0**).

Mark your answers **on the separate answer sheet**.

BRITAIN'S WILDEST PLACE

by Jon Orchard-Smith

It was just after 5 a.m. and the summer sun was rising over the mountains as the *Marguerite Explorer* sailed out of the loch into the calm waters of the sea. I was at the wheel – under the watchful eye of the captain. A few of the other dozen passengers and crew were on deck, clutching mugs of coffee. **0** **H** In the morning light, a dozen dolphins, grey and graceful, were swimming straight towards us.

The Hebrides, a group of islands off the Scottish coast, offer tourists a diversity of wildlife and scenery with few equals in the UK. **16** In places it is possible to see such marine animals from the shore, but to have the best views, you need to be on a boat.

17 The *Marguerite Explorer* was the first boat to offer whale-watching holidays throughout the Hebrides. Under the command of Christopher Swann, the crew of the *Marguerite* have worked with some of the world's leading sea-life scientists. They are very knowledgeable guides to the islands.

The Hebridan archipelago stretches nearly 250 miles from top to bottom, covers over a hundred miles from side to side, and has about 2,500 miles of coastline. **18** This relative lack of people, together with freedom from pollution, helps to make the Hebrides a haven for rare flowers and plants.

19 Some of the islands are under threat from mining and throughout the islands, developments such as fish farms, which are vital to the local economy, affect the environment too.

The Hebrides have their share of problems, but they are unbelievably beautiful. Why, then, aren't they packed with tourists? While visitors are an increasingly important part of the island economy, tourism is still low key, compared with some other parts of Britain. The answer may be that the prevailing Hebridan climate is wet and windy. **20**

Another discouraging factor is the wildlife the tourists least want to see – the insects, especially the mosquitoes. Particularly between July and September, visitors can expect to be severely bitten. Like so many wild places, the Hebrides can be hard on visitors. **21** And you will feel you will want to return to them, as I felt when I approached the end of my journey in the *Marguerite Explorer*.

A There are now a number of companies offering such trips.

B However, only about 40 out of the hundreds of islands are permanently inhabited.

C This is more than enough to put off the casual guest.

D And in the waters around them you can find not only dolphins but whales and the mighty sea eagle as well.

E But once you've watched dolphins leap through the dazzling water around your boat, you'll think they are paradise.

F Moreover, the fate of the islands and their people are bound together.

G Despite being relatively unspoilt, the Hebrides are also facing many pressures.

H Suddenly someone shouted: a splash in the water, half a mile away.

You are going to read an article about the artists who draw animated cartoons. For Questions **22–35**, choose from the people (**A–D**). The people may be chosen more than once. There is an example at the beginning (**0**).

Mark your answers **on the separate answer sheet**.

A	Dan Taylor
B	Colin Grey
C	David Hoxton
D	Carl Hughes

Which artist

used to consider drawing was a pastime?	**0**	*A*
went abroad to find work?	**22**	
helped an arts school financially?	**23**	
thinks the ability to tell a good story is essential?	**24**	
thinks people who are good at drawing find jobs easily?	**25**	
thinks computers will replace skilled cartoonists?	**26**	
wants to attract adult audiences?	**27**	
says some artists are afraid of losing independence?	**28**	
thinks art schools do not teach students basic skills?	**29**	
runs a course for trainees?	**30**	
says many good cartoon artists work in advertising?	**31**	
will display his work for the public to see?	**32**	
likes being part of a large team?	**33**	
used to do drawings for colleagues?	**34**	
has invested in new equipment?	**35**	

Tip Strip

- You do not need to read the whole text first.
- Read each question and underline the key words.
- Read the text quickly and find the information. Remember the text is long and contains information which you will not need.
- When you find the relevant part of the text, read it carefully.
- Questions and text will not contain the same words. You need to look for the meaning, e.g. Question 23 'helped financially' = 'has given funds'.

Question 22: 'went abroad'. Be careful! The answer is not in paragraph 4.
Question 26: Look for a similar way of saying 'will replace'.
Question 29: Look for a similar way of saying 'basic skills'.

Jobs in cartoon animation

The future seems bright for animators, the artists who can make cartoons come to life. Four cartoonists give their impressions.

Dan Taylor is delighted that TV shows are now often inhabited by 'animated' cartoon characters. 'On paper the character you create is just a drawing,' he says, 'but then you give it movement, and it becomes a real TV personality.' Dan passed his art exams when he was at secondary school, but for many years he treated his drawing as a hobby. He would create images for his work mates, to be stuck on motorbikes or leather jackets. Eventually, he signed up at the Arts Institute to start a career as an animator. 'There is plenty of work around for people who can draw because cartoon shows can win sizeable audiences around the world,' he says. Dan would like to create cartoons that cross the boundary from children's animation to animated characters for grown-ups, with issues that interest them. Many of his ideas for future series will be on show at the annual animation festival in Bradford next September.

As head of animation of Grant Studios, **Colin Grey** sees his work load grow day by day. 'There is a huge public taste for animation,' he says, 'but we still lack skilled artists because the publicity industry has employed lots of people who are now busy designing ads.' Recognising the need to encourage training, Grey has just given some funds to the university for an arts school qualification in animation. 'This is a good investment of some of our profits,' he says. Grey believes another problem is that many animators are often reluctant to go for jobs in the big organisations. 'They fear large-scale projects will take away their freedom of action,' he says. He is trying to bring a bit more of the US way of working to bear on his current projects. 'Of course production methods have changed since Walt Disney put together his first animation. Now studios can create a character and have it animated in a different country.'

Despite the recent demand for cartoon artists in Europe, **David Hoxton** found that the only way to get his ideal job was to leave England and try his luck in the USA. 'Their way of working is with large numbers of people working on each series of drawings,' he says, 'I'd always dreamt of working in such a way, producing the thousands of drawings necessary to bring characters to life.' Hoxton thinks his job requires excellent drawing techniques, something he feels is often neglected in schools. 'Colleges of art encourage independent thinking, which is good, but some of them have lost their way when it comes to teaching the essentials.' He admits that computers can now do the translating of a drawing into a moving image, but he is convinced the skilled artist will always be in demand.

Carl Hughes is the owner and chief animator of Manton Hall Films, one of the biggest animator outfits in Europe. In the last three years, he has spent £10m on new machines to compete with international rivals. The reward has been a string of contracts to animate US shows at its offices in England. 'We believe training our staff is very important,' he says, 'I offer them a series of classes within a 12-week intensive programme. After that, they join the teams on particular shows.' Hughes believes what he needs most is artists who have artistic potential, not so much the ability to draw as the ability to develop the plot of a narrative, an interesting plot that will interest the audience. He knows that many people in the industry are crying out for highly-skilled animators to get involved in the development of shows, but he thinks the future of all that area of work lies with computers. 'Eventually they will do away with the need for artists,' he says.

PART 1   You **must** answer this question.

1   You are organising an adventure weekend holiday for a group of friends. You have seen the advertisement below, but you need to know more. Using the notes you have made, write to Adventure Weekend, giving relevant details and asking for further information.

experience needed?

Adventure Weekend

A DIFFERENT HOLIDAY...

● Mountain climbing, sailing, walking and many more options!

● Our prices include almost everything

● All you need to bring is appropriate clothes

● Send us details about your group's age, interests and level of fitness, and we can suggest the best adventure weekend for you …

canoeing?

food?

e.g.?

Write a **letter** of between **120** and **180** words in an appropriate style. Do not write any addresses.

Tip Strip

- You don't have to be imaginative. Read the instructions carefully and underline key words and phrases, e.g. <u>give relevant details</u> or <u>ask for further information</u>.
- Read the input material. What information does the advertisement ask for?
- Base your answer on the input material, but try to use your own words.
- Think about who you are writing to. Which style is best: more formal or less formal? Should you use *Yours sincerely*, *Yours faithfully* or *Best wishes*?
- Plan your answer. Paragraph 1: express your interest in the holiday and give information about your group; Paragraph 2: request the extra information about the holiday (based on the hand-written notes).
- When you've finished, read the input information again. Have you included everything?
- Check the word limit, but don't waste time counting every word.
- Check your grammar and spelling.

Write an answer to **one** of the Questions **2–5** in this part. Write your answer in **120–180** words in an appropriate style.

2   This is part of a letter you receive from an English friend.

> *In your last letter you said you were organising a surprise party for a friend. Was it difficult to organise? What did your friend say? I'd love to hear how it went.*

Write your **letter**, answering your friend's questions and giving relevant details. Do not write any addresses.

3   You have been asked to write a story for your school magazine. The story must **begin** like this:

Peter opened the door and saw Jack standing in the doorway. Jack had returned, and Peter was frightened.

Write your **story**.

4   A magazine for young people called *Pastimes* has asked you to write about your favourite hobby. Write an article, describing your hobby and explaining why you would recommend it to other readers.

Write your **article**.

5   Answer **one** of the following two questions based on your reading of **one** of the set books.

Either   (a)   'I don't like the way this story ends.' With reference to the book you have read, write a **composition**, saying whether you agree or disagree with this statement.

Or   (b)   Which character from the book do you feel could be your friend and why? Write a **composition**, describing the character you chose and saying why he/she could be your friend.

Tip Strip

- Read the questions carefully. Choose a question you have ideas and vocabulary for.
- Underline key points in the question and include them in your answer.
- Before you start writing, think of the main point you will include in each paragraph.
- Pay attention to organisation: all options require you to write in paragraphs.
- Check for spelling and grammar mistakes.

Question 2:
- Answer **all** your friend's questions.
- Use an informal style, but start and end the letter in an appropriate letter format.

Question 3:
- Think of how your story will develop **before** you start writing.
- Check your verb sequences, e.g. simple past / past perfect.
- Remember: no greeting, no headings.

Question 4:
- Use a neutral style, you do not know the reader.
- Introduce your topic in the first paragraph and summarise what you have said in your final paragraph.
- You are asked to <u>describe</u> your hobby and <u>explain</u> why you recommend it. Use vocabulary related to hobbies and leisure, and the language of description, opinion and explanation.
- Avoid repeating the same adjectives, e.g. nice, good.

Question 5(a):
- Say why you agree or disagree using examples from the book/story.
- Make notes on what to include in each paragraph **before** you start writing.
- Use a neutral to formal style.

Question 5(b):
- Describe a character **and** say why …. You can answer both parts in different paragraphs or combine both in each paragraph. Your answer should be a balance of both elements.

Use of English (1 hour 15 minutes)

For Questions **1–15**, read the text below and decide which answer **A**, **B**, **C** or **D** best fits each space. There is an example at the beginning (**0**).

Mark your answers **on the separate answer sheet**.

Tip Strip

- Read the text for general understanding.
- A, B, C, D are all grammatically possible, but only one fits the gap.
- The word must fit in the context of the text as a whole.
- Check the words before and after the gap. Some words can only be used with certain prepositions, some words will be part of set expressions.
- Read through the text and check that your answers make sense.

Question 2: Which verbs are usually used with 'role'? Which one is best in this context?

Question 5: Which phrasal verb means 'release'?

Question 7: All these words can follow 'in', but only one makes sense in this sentence.

Question 10: Which word completes the linking expression with 'what'?

Question 13: Which of the words is often found after the preposition 'under'?

Example:

0   **A** dating   **B** ageing   **C** growing   **D** stretching

0	A	B	C	D
	▭	▢	▢	▢

TREES FOR LIFE

Trees are amongst the biggest and longest-living things on Earth, some (**0**) ..... back longer than the oldest buildings. But (**1**) ..... being nice to look at, trees also (**2**) ..... an important role in improving the quality of our lives.

On a world-wide (**3**) ....., forests help to slow down the effects of global warming by using up the gas (**4**) ..... as carbon dioxide and giving (**5**) ..... the oxygen we need to breathe. At local neighbourhood level, trees also (**6**) ..... important environmental benefits. They offer shade and shelter, which in (**7**) ..... reduces the amount of energy needed to heat and cool (**8**) ..... buildings; at the same time, they also remove other impurities from the air we breathe.

Urban trees are especially important because for many people they provide the only daily (**9**) ..... with the natural world. What's (**10**) ....., urban trees also provide a home for birds, small animals and butterflies. (**11**) ..... the trees we would lose the pleasure of seeing these creatures in our cities. Regrettably, (**12**) ....., trees in cities are now coming under (**13**) ...... There is a limit to the level of pollution they can (**14**) ..... and, down at street level, their roots are being seriously (**15**) ..... by the digging needed to make way for modern telephone, television and other cables.

1	**A** as far as	**B** as long as	**C** as soon as	**D** as well as
2	**A** play	**B** show	**C** act	**D** serve
3	**A** scale	**B** size	**C** range	**D** area
4	**A** called	**B** known	**C** titled	**D** referred
5	**A** in	**B** away	**C** up	**D** out
6	**A** bring	**B** make	**C** take	**D** find
7	**A** turn	**B** place	**C** order	**D** reach
8	**A** opposite	**B** close	**C** next	**D** nearby
9	**A** junction	**B** touch	**C** contact	**D** taste
10	**A** more	**B** else	**C** most	**D** other
11	**A** Throughout	**B** Beyond	**C** Without	**D** Outside
12	**A** therefore	**B** whilst	**C** however	**D** despite
13	**A** risk	**B** threat	**C** danger	**D** warning
14	**A** stand in for	**B** face up to	**C** put up with	**D** fall back on
15	**A** concerned	**B** disturbed	**C** interfered	**D** involved

For Questions **16–30**, read the text below and think of the word which best fits each space. Use only **one** word in each space. There is an example at the beginning (**0**).

Write your answers **on the separate answer sheet**.

Example:	0	*take*

FIT FOR SPORTS

It's not always easy to decide which sport to (**0**) .... up. When choosing, it is important to remember that excellence in sports results (**16**) .... a number of factors. For some sports, the body shape and structure with (**17**) .... you are born are important. Top runners are typical examples of individuals (**18**) .... have selected a sport because of their natural body type. Many other sports are more dependent (**19**) .... training and technique, and anyone following a well-structured and appropriate training programme should do well.

The aim of all sports training (**20**) .... to improve fitness and skills, and to develop training programmes that are both safe (**21**) .... effective. To do (**22**) .... properly, an understanding of (**23**) .... physical demands of sport is needed. All sports require a combination of strength, speed, endurance, agility and flexibility to varying degrees. (**24**) .... is important is how these elements are combined to build up the skills of the sport (**25**) .... question. Other factors to be (**26**) .... into account in a training programme are diet, the importance of avoiding injuries, your general state of health, and the nature and role (**27**) .... other team players.

Bearing (**28**) .... considerations in mind, anyone prepared to work (**29**) .... it can expect to progress to a very reasonable competitive level, even (**30**) .... only a few people will go on to break world records.

Tip Strip

- Read the text for general understanding.
- The word must make sense in the context of the text as a whole.
- Decide which type of word each gap needs, e.g. preposition, relative, conjunction, verb, adverb, etc.
- Look out for fixed expressions, dependent prepositions after certain verbs and linking words and phrases.
- Read through the text and check that your answers make sense.

Question 16: What type of word goes here? Which two words are possible? Which one makes most sense with what comes before and after?
Question 18: Which type of word goes here? Are 'individuals' places, people or things?
Question 20: The writer is talking about something in general. Which tense should be used?
Question 28: The word you need refers back to the last paragraph. Is it singular or plural?

For Questions **31–40**, complete the second sentence so that it has a similar meaning to the first sentence, using the word given. **Do not change the word given.** You must use between two and five words, including the word given. Here is an example (**0**).

Example: **0**   You must write all you personal details on this form.

fill

You must .... with all your personal details.

The gap can be filled by the words 'fill in this form' so you write:

0	*fill in this form*

Write **only the missing words** on the separate answer sheet.

Tip Strip

- Look at the **key word**. What type of word is it? What usually follows it, e.g. an infinitive, a gerund, a pronoun?
- Write your answer **on the question paper** and read **both** sentences again. Make sure that you haven't added any extra information.
- Write only the missing words on the answer sheet.
- Check your spelling.
- Contracted words count as two words, e.g. don't = do not.

Question 31: Which verb form follows 'wish'?

Question 32: Reported speech: what word follows 'advise'?

Question 34: Active to Passive: make sure you keep to the same verb tense.

Question 36: Present perfect to Past simple: what word do you need instead of 'for'?

Question 38: Be careful with the 3rd person singular in your answer.

31 I'd love to go on holiday in March, but that's my busiest month.

   wish

   I .... go on holiday in March, but that's my busiest month.

32 'Harry, I think you should cancel the concert if this rain continues,' John said.

   advised

   John .... the concert if the rain continued.

33 Not many students attended Dr Brown's lecture on politics.

   number

   Only .... students attended Dr Brown's lecture on politics.

34 City residents are going to organise a campaign to reduce street noise.

   be

   A campaign to reduce street noise .... by city residents.

35 After the accident Brenda was confused and did not recognise her brother.

   so

   After the accident Brenda .... did not recognise her brother.

36 Peter hasn't seen his aunt Lucy for years.

   saw

   It's .... his aunt Lucy.

37 The police said John had stolen the money.

   accused

   The police .... the money.

38 Tania has a mobile phone because her son may need to contact her.

   in case

   Tania has a mobile phone .... to contact her.

39 The reason Gloria didn't tell us the truth is that she was afraid of our reaction.

   if

   Gloria would have told us the truth .... afraid of our reaction.

40 The students organised a show but they postponed it due to lack of funds.

   put

   The students organised a show but they .... of lack of funds.

For Questions **41–55**, read the text below and look carefully at each line. Some of the lines are correct, and some have a word which should not be there.

If a line is correct, put a tick (✔) by the number **on the separate answer sheet**. If a line has a word which should not be there, write the word **on the separate answer sheet**. There are examples at the beginning (**0** and **00**).

Tip Strip

- Read the text for general understanding.
- Not more than five lines are correct.
- Look at the whole sentence, not just at the numbered lines.
- Underline words you think are wrong and read the sentence (not the line) without it. Does it sound right?
- Look out for extra pronouns. There are two examples in this text. Can you find them?
- Incorrect words can only occur **once** in a line.

Line 41: Is it a preposition, a pronoun or a conjunction which isn't needed here?

Lines 45–46: Find the grammatical mistake in this sentence. What time is referred to?

Line 48: Is there something here twice?

Examples:	0	*of*
	00	✔

0	....	On lovely sunny days in the summer, many of people in London
00	....	go along to one of the beautiful parks. Most of them go there
41	....	just to sit around and relax themselves with friends, but I prefer
42	....	something such more active. For me, one of the most exciting
43	....	things to do is flying a kite. It's amazing how much fun you
44	....	can have with a small and piece of material on a long piece of
45	....	cord. The best thing about kites is that, unless you will want
46	....	one that can do lots of fancy tricks to impress your friends,
47	....	they don't cost a very lot of money. You need a day when
48	....	there's a good strong breeze. To get it the kite flying, you have
49	....	to unwind a few metres of the cord and then get a friend to
50	....	hold the kite up while you to get a good grip on the handles.
51	....	Then, you start running towards the wind, that making sure your
52	....	friend lets go at the more right moment. As the wind catches
53	....	the kite, unwind the cord and watch the kite climb by higher
54	....	and higher. Keep a good hold so you don't lose it and, of
55	....	course, avoid trees, unless you're be good at climbing!

For Questions **56–65**, read the text below. Use the word given in capitals at the end of each line to form a word that fits in the space in the same line. There is an example at the beginning (**0**). Write your answers **on the separate answer sheet**.

Example: | **0** | *explorer* |

FLORIDA

When the famous (**0**) ...*explorer*...., Columbus claimed Florida for Spain in   **EXPLORE**
1492, he had never (**56**) .... eyes on it. The area's most important   **LAY**
early (**57**) .... thus set a pattern that has continued for centuries.   **VISIT**
There is a general (**58**) .... amongst people, apparently quite   **BELIEVE**
(**59**) .... with whether or not they've been there themselves, that   **CONNECT**
Florida is a good place to go.

In fact, it is almost (**60**) .... not to enjoy yourself in Florida today,   **POSSIBLE**
given the wonderful (**61**) .... of facilities available to tourists. Some   **SELECT**
of the world's most popular tourist (**62**) .... are located in the state   **ATTRACT**
whose (**63**) .... beaches welcome 40 million people each year.   **SAND**
These days it seems (**64**) .... to describe Florida's geography and   **POINT**
climate. After all, few people would have (**65**) .... in finding it on a   **DIFFICULT**
map and most would know what weather to expect there.

Tip Strip

- Read the text for general understanding.
- Decide what type of word you need for each gap (e.g. noun, adjective, etc.).
- Look at the whole sentence, not just at the line containing the gap.
- You should make no more than two changes to the word.
- You may need to add a prefix or suffix to some words.
- Some words may be positive or negative. Check the meaning of the passage!
- Read through the text and check that your words make sense.
- Check your spelling.

Question 56: What's the past participle of this word?
Question 58: Is a noun, verb or adjective needed here?
Question 62: Is this word going to be singular or plural?
Question 64: Read the text to the end. Is this word going to express a negative or positive idea? Will you add a prefix or a suffix?

Listening (40 minutes)

You will hear people talking in eight different situations. For Questions **1–8**, choose the best answer **A**, **B** or **C**.

Tip Strip

- Read the **question** before the options and underline key words.
- Each question is based on a different listening text with a separate mark.
- Relax and concentrate on each new text, don't think of the one you have just done.
- Decide on one of the options after the first listening.
- Use the second listening to check that you are correct.
- If you are not sure, guess. You may have understood more than you think.
- Do not listen for single words, but for the general meaning.
- Don't worry about words that you don't know.

Question 3: The listening text mentions paint, photography and stone figures, but which are in the collection?

Question 4: What can be learnt as you go along?

Question 5: The customer has a guide book, but does he use it?

1 You hear part of a radio play.
Where does this scene take place?
A in a restaurant
B at a police station
C in the street

1

2 You turn on the radio and hear a man talking.
What are you listening to?
A a competition
B a lesson
C an advertisement

2

3 You hear a woman talking about an exhibition.
What can you see in the exhibition?
A paintings
B photographs
C sculptures

3

4 You hear a manager talking about the skills young employees need.
What skills are essential in his opinion?
A problem-solving skills
B writing skills
C computer skills

4

5 You hear a hotel manager talking to a customer.
Where did the customer get the information about the hotel?
A from a guide book
B from the Internet
C from a friend

5

6 You hear a young girl who spent a month in a foreign country talking about her experience.
What was good about it?
A She became self-confident.
B She improved her language skills.
C She travelled to many places.

6

7 You hear a woman talking about a book on the radio.
What is the book about?
A healthy eating habits
B the history of food
C teenagers and food

7

8 You hear a young woman giving advice on going night clubbing.
What is her advice?
A Think about what you will wear.
B Be prepared for extra expenses.
C Check the music is what you like.

8

You will hear an interview with the dancer, Darren Faiweather. For Questions **9–18**, complete the sentences.

Darren's father thought that dancing classes would enable him to

[_____ **9**] well.

The idea of dancing classes came from a [_____ **10**] who lived nearby.

Darren was successful as a dancer in both local and national

[_____ **11**]

In London, Darren found it difficult to [_____ **12**] at the College of Dance.

Darren worked in the college [_____ **13**] to pay for his classes.

As Darren lived outside London, he spent as long as

[_____ **14**] each day travelling.

Darren describes Lily Partridge as a [_____ **15**] teacher.

Darren thinks that Lily liked him because they often had

[_____ **16**]

Darren first became famous dancing in a ballet called [_____ **17**]

Darren is now well-known as a dancer who likes to perform

[_____ **18**]

PART 3

You will hear five different women talking on the subject of happiness. For Questions **19–23**, choose from the list **A–F** what each speaker says. Use the letters only once. There is one extra letter which you do not need to use.

A   She talks about her good news.

B   She starts each day with a decision.

C   She laughs at every opportunity.

D   She praises the people she likes.

E   She finds time for extra leisure activities.

F   She concentrates on a few activities.

Speaker 1	**19**
Speaker 2	**20**
Speaker 3	**21**
Speaker 4	**22**
Speaker 5	**23**

Tip Strip

- There are five different speakers talking on a similar topic. You hear all five once, then all five repeated.
- Read the instructions carefully. What will the people be talking about?
- Before you listen, read options A to F.
- On the first listening, note down the speaker's main idea. Mark the option closest to this idea.
- On the second listening, check your answers. You may need to change some of them.

Sometimes a word in the prompt occurs in several extracts, for example:
A: 'Good news' is mentioned by speakers 1 and 4, but neither 'talk about good news'. Listen for another way of saying this.
C: Laughing is mentioned by four of the speakers. But which speaker laughs a lot?
D: Speaker 2 mentions that people 'praise' her. But which speaker praises other people?

You will hear an interview with the television actor, Simon McGregor. For each of the Questions **24–30**, choose the best answer **A**, **B** or **C**.

Tip Strip

- The questions follow the order of the text.
- Before you listen, read through the questions and underline key words.
- Listen to find the answer to the question, then choose the option (A, B or C) which is closest.
- The words in the options will be different from the words you hear.
- Most questions will be about people's ideas, opinions, feelings, etc.

Question 24: 'Reason' is the most important word here. What does Simon say he lacked?

Question 25: Listen for the adjective Simon uses to describe his first job.

Question 27: Why is 'busking' in commas? This word is probably explained on the tape.

Question 29: What does 'According to Simon' mean?

Question 30: Whose opinion are we listening for here?

24 What reason does Simon give for not going into acting straight from school?

    A He didn't want to study any more.
    B He was not brave enough.
    C He lacked the necessary qualifications.

        24

25 How does Simon feel now about the careers advice he was given?

    A He is grateful for the opportunity it gave him.
    B He regrets not mentioning his real ambitions.
    C He wishes he hadn't trained as an accountant.

        25

26 What led Simon to give up accountancy?

    A He found the work boring.
    B He had developed other interests.
    C He realised he wasn't going to qualify.

        26

27 Why did Simon take up 'busking'?

    A to earn extra pocket money
    B to pay the fees for his course of study
    C to support himself while he studied

        27

28 How did Simon's grandmother influence him?

    A She encouraged him in his ambitions.
    B She organised plays for children.
    C She had been involved in the theatre.

        28

29 According to Simon, people who are shy

    A prefer to be on their own.
    B really want to be accepted.
    C find acting comes easily to them.

        29

30 Simon thinks that it is better for actors if they

    A can identify with the characters they play.
    B have to work hard to convince audiences.
    C are not too similar to the characters they play.

        30

PAPER 5

Speaking (14 minutes)

PART 1 (3 minutes)

The examiner will ask you both to talk briefly about yourselves by answering questions such as:

Where are you from? Tell us something about the area where you live.
What type of work do people do in your area?
What is there for young people to do in your area?

PART 2 (3 or 4 minutes)

You will each be asked to talk for a minute without interruption. You will each have two different photographs to talk about. You will also have to answer a question after your partner has spoken.

Newspapers (compare, contrast and speculate)

Turn to pictures 1 and 2 on page 151 which show people reading newspapers.

Candidate A, compare and contrast these photographs, and say why you think the people are reading newspapers. You have a minute to do this.

Candidate B, do you often read newspapers?

Parents and children (compare, contrast and speculate)

Turn to pictures 1 and 2 on page 152 which show parents and children.

Candidate B, compare and contrast these photographs, and say how you think the people are feeling about each other. You have a minute to do this.

Candidate A, did you often get into trouble as a child?

PART 3 (3 or 4 minutes)

You will be asked to discuss something together without interruption by the examiner. You will have a page of pictures to help you.

Jobs in television (discuss and evaluate)

Turn to the pictures on page 153 which show different jobs students could do in a television company to gain work experience.

How popular do you think these jobs might be with young people? In which two jobs would they learn the most useful skills?

PART 4 (3 or 4 minutes)

The examiner encourages you to develop the discussion in Part 3 by asking questions such as:

Would you like to work for a television company? Why (not)?
Why are people worried if children watch a lot of television?
How much are we influenced by what we see on television?
What do you think of television programmes for young people in this country?

Tip Strip

Part 1

• The examiner will ask you questions in turn. Don't try to learn a little speech about yourself. This will not answer the examiner's questions properly.

Part 2

• A minute is quite a long time to talk. Don't panic, don't go too fast.
• Don't interrupt your partner's turn. Listen so you can comment afterwards.
• Don't give separate descriptions of each picture. Compare and contrast them from the beginning.
• If you don't know a word in one of the pictures, describe what you mean using other words.

Part 3

• Ask your partner for his/her opinions, don't just say what you think.
• You have to talk for 3 minutes, so don't decide or agree too soon – talk about all the pictures first.
• You don't have to agree with your partner.

Part 4

• The examiner may ask you questions in turn, or may ask general questions for you both to answer.
• You don't have to agree with your partner, but try not to interrupt; let your partner finish, then say what you think.

TEST 2

Reading (1 hour 15 minutes)

You are going to read an article about a man who works as a professional shopper. Choose from the list **A–H** the sentence which best summarises each part (**1–6**) of the article. There is one extra sentence which you do not need to use. There is an example at the beginning (**0**).

Mark your answers **on the separate answer sheet**.

A	Bryan successfully avoids some of the problems that shoppers encounter.
B	Bryan's success may be related to a recognised trend.
C	Bryan's experience allows him to predict bargains.
D	Bryan makes his terms and conditions clear.
E	Bryan's initial success was not anticipated.
F	Bryan's clients are offered special treatment in shops.
G	Bryan's strategy is to provide a flexible service.
H	Bryan feels fortunate that he is able to combine work with pleasure.

Tip Strip

Another task in Part 1 asks you to match summary sentences to parts of an article.
- Read the text for general understanding.
- Read each paragraph, decide what the main point is, then find the sentence which is the best summary of it.
- The sentences won't use the same words as the text.

Sentence B talks about a 'trend'. Which paragraph talks about things which are changing?
Sentence D talks about 'terms and conditions'. Which paragraph describes what you get for your money if you use Bryan's service?
Sentence G says that Bryan's service is 'flexible'. Which paragraph tells us about different ways in which Bryan's service will help you?

THE GOOD BUY MAN

So, you don't want to get your toes crushed in the summer sales? Michele Dalton meets a man who'll do your shopping for you.

0	*H*

Bryan Bonaparte is that rare find – a man who loves shopping. Indeed, he loves it so much that he's set up an agency to provide a shopping service for those people who don't share his enthusiasm. 'I get a real buzz out of shopping,' admits Bryan. 'It's a challenge to track down what people want and to find new and interesting things on their behalf. People say to me, "I can't believe you enjoy doing this", but I do. And it's great to get paid for it as well.'

1	

Bryan's agency, called Ace, started in a small way one Christmas. It was meant to be just a seasonal thing, but it turned out to be so successful that he carried on throughout the year. It seems there are always gifts to buy for weddings, birthdays, anniversaries and retirements.

2	

A survey published in the *London Evening News* last year found that many people are getting increasingly depressed at the prospect of shopping, and this may go some way to explaining Bryan's success. The survey pinpointed crowds, bad weather, choosing the right present and carrying heavy bags as stress triggers.

3	

Planning a shopping trip with military precision is Bryan's solution. 'A lot of people go shopping, especially during the sales, with no idea what they are looking for,' he explains. 'It's no wonder they find wandering around the stores frustrating and exhausting.'

4	

The shopping stretch covered by Ace runs through most of London's West End shopping districts. Bryan, or another member of his team, is happy to take anyone shopping within this area or to visit stores on their behalf, delivering goods to clients' homes or offices at a convenient time, including evenings and weekends. If you don't actually know what you want, Ace will make suggestions, buy the items, then return to the shops to exchange them if you are not completely satisfied.

5	

A flat charge of £15 per hour applies to either service. Clients with a list of requests are given a quote based on the amount of time involved. The only thing Bryan won't do is buy food. For sales shopping, customers need to be specific about size, colour, style and designer labels. Details about the normal price and the discount that clients want are required, and Bryan warns that shops generally won't exchange items bought in sales.

6	

Bryan's specialist knowledge means that clients usually get a good deal. 'I've come to know how long the sales will run for, the stock that will be carried and whether old stock will be brought back in at sale time. If I know the store will reduce prices after a month, then I'll hang on before buying. Sometimes, prices can be slashed by up to 70% a few days before the sale ends. With Bryan to guide you, will shopping ever be the same again?

PART 2 You are going to read a magazine article about an artist. For Questions **7–14**, choose the correct answer **A**, **B**, **C** or **D**.

Mark your answers **on the separate answer sheet**.

The Ballet Sculptor

Delicate figures ready to begin a dance or caught in mid-flight – these images dominate the work of sculptor Suzy Jordan

Young sculptor Suzy Jordan is fast developing an international reputation for her beautifully-crafted figures which are made from a mixture of clay and metal. People love dancers, particularly ballet dancers, and Suzy has a fascination for them too. 'I used to long to be a dancer when I was younger,' she says. 'There's something amazing about all those graceful movements that, unknown to the audience, can be so painful for the dancers. I'm glad I didn't go in for it, but just watching them gives me so many ideas.'

Suzy has been in touch with some leading ballet companies to see if they'll allow her to sit and draw their dancers during rehearsal time. Her dream is to join forces with them, do a series of life-size sculptures and then hold an exhibition in the foyer of the theatre where the dancers perform.

Most of her sculpture is of figures. 'If I get the chance to sculpt from life, it's really great because I can work more quickly and I'm not guessing shapes or turning to reference books,' she told us. But most of her work has to be done from drawings. After graduating from Art School, Suzy taught drawing for a number of years before setting up as a sculptor, so at least she has the necessary skills.

Most of Suzy's works are individually commissioned and one piece can take as long as four or five months to complete. All of the work is done in a small shed in the garden of her family home in the country. This tin space, about 3 square metres, contains her main **worktop**, plus all her other gear. Suzy uses terracotta clay to form her sculptures and applies a mixture of lacquer and crushed metal powder, usually bronze, on top. This makes her pieces less expensive than solid bronze figures would be. She then adds a layer of resin or wax to give her work an aged look.

One of Suzy's biggest commissions came from a school in Sweden. They wanted three specially-designed life-size figures to suspend from the ceiling in their gymnasium. Hard to imagine how she did **it**, but each one was made in her garden shed. They had to be made of plaster so that they wouldn't be too heavy to hang up. Suzy travelled to Sweden with the sculptures to help direct their installation. One of the drawbacks of working to commissions rather than on mass produced pieces is having to work out what sort of price to charge. 'I used to be such a softie,' she confides. 'If someone fell in love with something I'd made, I'd accept a lower offer or let them pay for it in instalments, just so that it went to a good home. But I've learnt not to do that anymore.'

Suzy's work starts at around £100 for the smallest figures, but large sculptures can cost as much as £3000 each. But as she doesn't make copies of her work, each person has an original, so they must be worth having as an investment. As she explains, 'All artists want some kind of recognition for their work. I don't think many of us do it for the money. I have a friend who says she can't wait to see my work in ten years and see how it's progressed. I'm very lucky to be doing the sort of work where that kind of progression shows.'

7 How does Suzy feel about dancers?

    A inspired by the way they move
    B upset by how much they suffer
    C sad that she didn't train to be one
    D impressed by how they react to audiences

8 Suzy has contacted certain ballet companies because she'd like to

    A find a job in a theatre.
    B sell sculptures to them.
    C be invited to performances.
    D co-operate in a joint project.

9 Why would Suzy prefer not to work from drawings?

    A She's not good at drawing.
    B Books advise against it.
    C It takes a long time to do.
    D She'd like to develop new skills.

10 What is a 'worktop' (line 29)?

    A a type of building
    B a piece of equipment
    C a surface to work on
    D an article of clothing

11 Why does Suzy not make her figures wholly from metal?

    A They would look too new.
    B They would cost too much.
    C It would make them too heavy.
    D It would require more space.

12 What does 'it' in line 39 refer to?

    A producing the figures
    B designing the figures
    C delivering the figures
    D hanging the figures

13 Why has Suzy's attitude towards her work changed?

    A She now produces larger quantities.
    B She now only works to commission.
    C She no longer has problems selling it.
    D She has become more businesslike.

14 What does Suzy find satisfying about her work?

    A Each piece is unique.
    B She makes a good living.
    C Her work is rising in value.
    D People appreciate what she does.

You are going to read a magazine article about a man who works as a diver. Six paragraphs have been removed from the article. Choose the most suitable paragraph from the list **A–H** for each part (**15–20**). There is one extra paragraph which you do not need to use. There is an example at the beginning (**0**).

Mark your answers **on the separate answer sheet**.

THE GOLFBALL FROGMAN

Professional diver Adam Tranter was thrilled when some friends invited him for a round of golf at an internationally famous course. If he did well, he might be allowed to join the socially-prestigious golf club.

0	H

Unwilling to give up the idea of joining the golf club altogether, Adam hit upon the idea of using his diving skills to make himself useful. He put on his wetsuit, strapped a couple of air tanks to his back, and began retrieving lost balls from the lakes on the course.

15	

And you can't really blame them because there is something a bit ridiculous about a grown man wandering around a golf course in a rubber suit and goggles, jumping into ponds. But for Adam it's a serious business and, apparently, he's also providing a valuable service to golfers.

16	

Of course, Adam does also come across less distinguished balls and plenty that look a bit knocked-about. These also have a price, however, he cleans them up and sells them at second-hand sales and to other less prestigious golf clubs.

17	

Most of the lakes are only five or six feet deep, but on the bottom it's impossible to see a thing, you just have to feel around in the mud for the balls. Adam has to be very careful too, because you get all sorts of things down there – bottles, cans, all sorts of junk. If he were to cut himself, he could be out of action for weeks.

18	

Fortunately, Adam's never been in any kind of difficulty. Nonetheless, he always has someone with him, keeping watch just in case. 'A golf course can be a fairly lonely place,' he explains. 'You can be a long way from help should you ever need it.'

19	

Despite all these hazards, Andrew insists that the job is great fun. 'I was under a lot of weed a couple of weeks ago and all you could make out from the surface was my air tank. A young guy, searching the banks of the lake for his ball, spotted me and ran to the clubhouse shouting, "There's a monster in the lake!" '

20	

Luckily, nobody at the club has complained about Adam's activities, however, and one suspects that given his notoriety in the golfing world, his membership is now secure.

Another task in Part 3 asks you to insert paragraphs into an article.

- Read through the base text for general understanding.
- Read the text around each gap carefully. Look at the whole paragraph, before and after the gap.
- Read paragraphs A–H. Check for topic and language links with paragraphs in the base text.
- Reread the text and the paragraphs to check that it makes sense.

Paragraph B talks about 'another such danger'. Which paragraph in the base text talks about dangerous things?

Paragraph D begins with 'But'. It is making a contrast with something in the previous piece of text. Which paragraph in the base text tells us something about money?

Paragraph G talks about 'people' and their reaction to Adam's job. Which paragraph in the base text explains why this happens? It uses a pronoun instead of 'people'.

A   He makes a good living out of it too. Adam can collect anything from 1,000 to 2,000 balls during a day's diving. A lot of them are good quality with hardly a mark on them and can be sold to professional golfing shops, which in turn sell them back to golfers.

B   Another such danger is weed. The water in the lakes tends to be stagnant and so plant matter tends to build up very quickly. A diver can easily get tangled up, therefore. Adam is well-aware of the danger and, as a professional, knows better than to take unnecessary chances.

C   Another thing to look out for is golf balls themselves. 'I usually dive while play is going on and quite often I can be in a lake when balls are landing in it,' says Adam. 'Getting hit by one of those things would be nobody's idea of a joke.'

D   But Adam wouldn't want us to get the impression that it's easy money. 'I don't want kids thinking that they can earn extra pocket money by doing this,' he insists. 'It is dangerous, dirty, cold and smelly.'

E   Apart from that, Adam has few regrets about his decision. Indeed, he has become more involved in the world of golf than he bargained for.

F   On another occasion, when he was covered in weed, he surfaced just behind some poor unsuspecting golfer and yelled 'Boo!' The poor man apparently went very white and no one has seen him at the golf club since.

G   As a result, Adam has become something of a celebrity on the golf courses of southern England – as a frogman. 'When I tell people what I do, they just fall about laughing,' he says.

H   It didn't take him long to realise, however, that although he was a natural in the water, he was quite out of his depth on the green. He had no future as a golfer.

You are going to read some interviews with women who have unusual jobs. For Questions **21–35**, choose from the people (**A–D**). The people may be chosen more than once. There is an example at the beginning (**0**).

Mark your answers **on the separate answer sheet**.

A	**Dina Dorset**
B	**Angela Bell**
C	**Claire Dorn**
D	**Dolly Masons**

Which interview is with someone who

works part-time?	**0**	*A*
had a better salary in an earlier job?	**21**	
cannot make friends at work?	**22**	
will get a university qualification?	**23**	
has to pretend she is always happy?	**24**	
writes to her customers?	**25**	
meets her customers socially?	**26**	
organises activities for older people?	**27**	
was promoted at work?	**28**	
does not like to use her voice?	**29**	
has a job that affects her health?	**30**	
had an earlier job as a teacher?	**31**	
thinks attitudes towards her work have changed?	**32**	
has the job she had always wanted?	**33**	
considers work more important than family?	**34**	
has responsibility for quality control?	**35**	

Women in unusual jobs

Dina Dorset

is a disc jockey in a night-club in London. A few years ago she thought her future was in tennis. 'For a while I trained promising young players on a full-time basis, but one day a neighbour who was a radio producer took me down to his radio station and I became involved in the music scene,' she says. There are lots of late nights for Dina but surprisingly the job doesn't offer her much in the way of a social life. 'I don't have any real contact with the large numbers of people I meet,' she says. She particularly likes the fact that she now only works four hours a day. 'The one thing I resent is having to appear cheerful all the time even when I feel down,' she says. She hopes to be able to produce her own records one day but she has given up her ambition of going to college. 'You can't do everything in life,' she says.

Angela Bell

is a clown, she paints her face white and wears funny clothes to entertain people. She decided clowning was the job she wanted after seeing a clown show. 'I said that was it. It involved no talking, and that suited me down to the ground,' she says. She soon realised that women only introduced the act and were on stage for a few minutes because it was considered a job for men. 'That is changing now,' she says. 'But from the beginning I decided to call myself Chris on the programmes instead of Angela so that the audience don't know if I'm a man or a woman.' Angela had to choose between family and work. 'I liked my work too much to think of children,' she says, 'and I have no regrets.' She says the secret of her success is that she is a very happy person, which is what you need to be a good clown.

Claire Dorn

works on a cruise liner, a floating luxury hotel which is her home for eight months of the year. She is the ship's secretary and has responsibility for all information customers may need while on board, as well as acting as secretary to the captain. 'He is very demanding but I have no complaints from him,' she says. Losing touch with the real world for so long is no problem because the ship's officers can take advantage of the activities provided for the entertainment of passengers. 'I've made many lasting friendships here,' she says, 'we get customers of all ages and backgrounds.' Her previous work experience as a Personal Assistant to a manager prepared her for the demands of this job. It was better paid than her present job but she gave it up because she had always liked the idea of working on a ship. 'The only disadvantage is that there are constant time changes when you go round the world and it makes you feel physically unwell,' she says.

Dolly Masons

has worked in a chocolate factory for the past twenty years. 'I was nearly sixteen when I joined,' she says. 'My parents both worked here at the time, so it had become a kind of family tradition. My first job was as an assistant and I've since climbed the ladder to become customer relations manager.' Her present job involves a number of responsibilities, from performing taste tests for all chocolates to ensure their flavour is the same, to organising events for retired employees, including parties and excursions to the seaside. 'I like to have variety in my job,' she says, 'any comments from customers will be forwarded to me to deal with. Of course, I'll never meet them personally but they will all get a written response from me.' She admits that at the moment she is finding it difficult to concentrate on the degree course in marketing she started last year, but is confident she will finish it by June.

PAPER 2   Writing (1 hour 30 minutes)

You **must** answer this question.

1   You and a friend want to find a summer job abroad. Your friend has sent you a letter with an advertisement. Read the letter and the advertisement together with the notes.

> This sounds interesting, just what we want. I've made some notes on it but I'm too busy with exams. Can you write to them for more details? Maybe you can think of other questions, too.
>
> See you soon

Write a letter to the Summer Jobs Agency asking for the information which your friend suggests and adding any relevant questions of your own.

Write a **letter** of between **120** and **180** words in an appropriate style. Do not write any addresses.

Write an answer to one of the Questions **2–5** in this part. Write your answer in **120–180** words in an appropriate style.

2   You have received this invitation from a magazine called 'Animal Life'.

> We have heard you know a lot about animals. Could you write an article for us explaining to our readers which animals make good pets and how to look after them?

Write your **article**.

3   You have been doing a class project on traditional festivals in your country. Now your teacher has asked you to write a composition on the following subject:

My favourite local festival

Write your **composition**.

4   You have just come back from a visit to a local museum organised by your school. The Principal has asked you to write a report about the museum and what you saw there, saying whether it is of interest for all age groups in the school.

Write a **report** for the Principal.

5   Answer **one** of the following two questions based on your reading of **one** of the set books.

Either   (a)   Write a **composition**, comparing two characters from the story you have read and saying which of the two you prefer and why.

Or   (b)   'I would have preferred to see this story on film and not to have read it.' With reference to the book you have read, write a **composition**, saying whether you agree or disagree with this statement and why.

Use of English (1 hour 15 minutes)

For Questions **1–15**, read the text below and decide which answer **A**, **B**, **C** or **D** best fits each space. There is an example at the beginning (**0**).

Mark your answers **on the separate answer sheet**.

Example:

0   **A**   became   **B**   turned   **C**   appeared   **D**   succeeded

---

POLAR ADVENTURER

In March 1999, Amyr Klink, a Brazilian yachtsman and polar adventurer, (**0**) ..... the first man to circle Antarctica while staying south of 50 degrees latitude. He (**1**) ..... the most dangerous sea route in the world. Klink was already (**2**) ..... known because in 1984 he had rowed across the Atlantic in a small boat. The book which he wrote, based on his (**3**) ..... on that trip, had by then (**4**) ..... millions of copies.

For his polar adventure, Klink built his (**5**) ..... boat. He (**6**) ..... off in 1998 from South Georgia and he arrived back there 88 days later – although he (**7**) ..... eleven of those days on dry land in Antarctica. He did not stop there out of (**8**) ....., but because he wanted to see the Antarctic Peninsula.

Klink knew that his (**9**) ..... would be dangerous. On the way he had to be careful to (**10**) ..... huge floating blocks of ice. These icebergs, as they are called, were everywhere and (**11**) ..... one of them would have been a disaster. As Klink knew that any rescue mission would have been impossible in the rough seas, he did not (**12**) ..... to take a life-boat.

When he sailed into (**13**) ..... winds 750 miles south of Tasmania, he met waves that were twenty-five metres high. This meant staying awake most of the time. He only managed to sleep for twenty-minute (**14**) ..... at a stretch. But he succeeded in the end, (**15**) ..... all the difficulties that he had to face.

1	**A**	went	**B**	took	**C**	had	**D**	made
2	**A**	really	**B**	widely	**C**	broadly	**D**	thoroughly
3	**A**	events	**B**	incidents	**C**	happenings	**D**	experiences
4	**A**	sold	**B**	printed	**C**	bought	**D**	produced
5	**A**	proper	**B**	individual	**C**	own	**D**	single
6	**A**	set	**B**	put	**C**	left	**D**	got
7	**A**	passed	**B**	lived	**C**	spent	**D**	remained
8	**A**	necessity	**B**	demand	**C**	urgency	**D**	requirement
9	**A**	excursion	**B**	tour	**C**	voyage	**D**	cruise
10	**A**	expect	**B**	avoid	**C**	escape	**D**	refuse
11	**A**	crashing	**B**	breaking	**C**	knocking	**D**	hitting
12	**A**	consider	**B**	mind	**C**	bother	**D**	accept
13	**A**	fast	**B**	strong	**C**	heavy	**D**	hard
14	**A**	periods	**B**	times	**C**	occasions	**D**	lengths
15	**A**	as far as	**B**	apart from	**C**	according to	**D**	in spite of

For Questions **16–30**, read the text below and think of the word which best fits each space. Use only **one** word in each space. There is an example at the beginning (**0**).

Write your answers **on the separate answer sheet**.

Example: | **0** | *at* |

GOOD AT LANGUAGES

At school, Sarah Biggs says she was very bad (**0**) .... languages. Now she speaks English, Spanish and Italian and works (**16**) .... a bilingual secretary in a travel company in England. (**17**) .... several foreign languages at work is not easy, but for Sarah, and other multi-lingual secretaries (**18**) .... her, it is all standard practice.

Sarah comes from Spain, (**19**) .... she attended school and college. But it was time spent abroad after college (**20**) .... encouraged her interest in languages.

In her job, Sarah has (**21**) .... great deal more responsibility than the title of secretary would suggest. She stresses the importance of (**22**) .... fluent in Spanish because part of her job is dealing (**23**) .... customers from Latin America. (**24**) .... such clients come from abroad, she has to translate everything (**25**) .... say into English. She is given (**26**) .... time for preparation at all, so this aspect of her job is one of the (**27**) .... difficult.

It is important for Sarah to be up-to-date with changes (**28**) .... her own language, so she reads Spanish newspapers and books looking for new additions to (**29**) .... vocabulary. Sarah says she (**30**) .... not give up this job even if they offered her a better salary in another company.

PART 3

For Questions **31–40**, complete the second sentence so that it has a similar meaning to the first sentence, using the word given. **Do not change the word given.** You must use between two and five words, including the word given. Here is an example (**0**).

Example: **0** All your lockers must be left completely empty at the end of term.

nothing

You must .... your lockers at the end of term.

The gap can be filled by the words 'leave nothing in' so you write:

0	leave nothing in

Write **only the missing words** on the separate answer sheet.

---

31 'Don't touch the cake, Toby, it's still hot,' said Mrs Smith.

not

Mrs Smith .... the cake because it was still hot.

32 Tamsin was the only student who hadn't done her homework.

apart

All the students .... done their homework.

33 I expect Lucy was pleased that she'd won the prize.

been

Lucy .... that she'd won the prize.

34 'I will only work extra hours if I get paid at a higher rate.'

unless

'I will .... I get paid at a higher rate.'

35 Max offered Gaby a lift to the station, but she didn't accept.

turned

Gaby .... offer of a lift to the station.

36 Valerie doesn't object to her photograph appearing in the magazine.

objection

Valerie .... her photograph appearing in the magazine.

37 There is no more petrol left in the car.

run

The car .... petrol.

38 'If you ask me, you should buy a new coat, Tracy,' said her mother.

advised

Tracy's mother .... a new coat.

39 People say that the famous couple are about to get married.

said

The famous couple .... about to get married.

40 You can borrow my camera, but you must be careful with it.

long

You can borrow my camera .... careful with it.

For Questions **41–55**, read the text below and look carefully at each line. Some of the lines are correct, and some have a word which should not be there.

If a line is correct, put a tick (✔) by the number **on the separate answer sheet**. If a line has a word which should not be there, write the word **on the separate answer sheet**. There are examples at the beginning (**0** and **00**).

Examples:	0	*it*
	00	✔

THIS IS MY HOBBY

0	....	If I had to say it what my hobby is, I suppose the answer would
00	....	have to be reading. It all started in early childhood when my
41	....	father used to enjoy much making up stories for my brother and
42	....	myself. This was a hugely popular every night at bedtime. As we
43	....	grew older, we turned to books and by the time I was ten, I had
44	....	a large collection of these children's literature. Ever since I can
45	....	remember, I have read about a book a week and I am get through
46	....	lots and lots of such magazines too. I especially enjoy reading in bed
47	....	and if I am really enjoying a book, I will stay up all night to finish it. But
48	....	I also tend to fill my spare up time with reading. You will often see
49	....	me reading on the bus, for example, or if I am waiting from in a queue.
50	....	I never go anywhere without have something to read. I actually
51	....	collect magazines and I have a room at home filled with them. I even
52	....	buy magazines written in languages that I don't know them, just for
53	....	the pleasure given of looking at the pictures and seeing the way
54	....	how they are designed. It will come as no great surprise, therefore,
55	....	if I will tell you that my main ambition in life is to become an editor.

For Questions **56–65**, read the text below. Use the word given in capitals at the end of each line to form a word that fits in the space in the same line. There is an example at the beginning (**0**). Write your answers **on the separate answer sheet**.

Example:	**0**	interested

THE TRAINING PROGRAMME

If you're (**0**) interested. in getting fit, then what you need is a training   **INTEREST**

programme. Although aimed at improving physical (**56**) ...., this   **FIT**

programme can also be (**57**) .... in such a way that it helps in the   **DESIGN**

(**58**) .... of particular athletic skills. There is a range of different   **DEVELOP**

(**59**) .... to choose from and a growing amount of scientific   **ACTIVE**

(**60**) .... to explain the effects of each one.   **KNOW**

When you begin training, it is important to start (**61**) ...., raising   **GENTLE**

the (**62**) .... of the programme in a gradual way. Although it is   **INTENSE**

important to work sufficiently hard to make an (**63**) .... on your   **IMPRESS**

physical condition, the activities shouldn't be (**64**) .... It is   **PAIN**

(**65**) ...., therefore, to ignore warning symptoms such as sharp or   **WISE**

persistent pain in particular muscles.

PAPER 4

Listening (40 minutes)

You will hear people talking in eight different situations. For Questions **1–8**, choose the best answer **A**, **B** or **C**.

1 You hear part of a play on the radio.
Who is the woman talking to?
  A her boss
  B her mother
  C her doctor

[ ] 1

2 You hear a man talking about a boat trip on a river.
What made this river dangerous?
  A its depth
  B its speed
  C its rocks

[ ] 2

3 You hear this advertisement on the radio.
What is the advertisement for?
  A a TV programme
  B a shop
  C a book

[ ] 3

4 You hear part of a play on the radio.
How does the man feel?
  A guilty
  B nervous
  C bored

[ ] 4

5 You are listening to the radio and hear this announcement.
What is the purpose of the announcement?
  A to complain about something
  B to praise someone's house
  C to recommend something

[ ] 5

6 You hear a man talking about the house where he lives.
What caused him problems in his bedroom?
  A the view from the window
  B the space for storing things
  C the heating system

[ ] 6

7 You hear a radio announcement about a future event.
What is the aim of the event?
  A promoting understanding of wildlife
  B developing electronic machinery
  C protecting the natural environment

[ ] 7

8 In a radio play, you hear this discussion about jigsaw puzzles.
Why does the man like jigsaw puzzles?
  A They help him to concentrate.
  B They help him to relax.
  C They help him to pass the time.

[ ] 8

You will hear someone welcoming students to an English School. For Questions **9–18**, complete the notes.

Tip Strip

Another task in Part 2 asks you to complete notes.

- Before you listen, read the questions. Think about the type of information which is missing.
- The words you need to write are on the tape.
- Write one to three words in each space.
- Check your spelling.

Question 9: Two places have the 'Guide to Activities' – the library and the reception. But only one of them has a copy available at the moment. Which is it?

Question 15: Two possible meeting places are mentioned, but where should students meet *this* Saturday?

Question 18: The teacher recommends one class, but recommends against another. Which one does she think students should do?

International English School

Guide to Activities: *available in* [_____ 9]

Course content: *conversation classes* * [_____ 10]

Problems with your course? *Go to* [_____ 11]

Activities organised:

Friday morning [_____ 12]

Friday afternoon [_____ 13]

For Saturday trip:

remember to bring [_____ 14]

meeting place [_____ 15]

Sunday 6 p.m.:

go to [_____ 16]

collect materials and [_____ 17]

Recommended extra class: [_____ 18]

You will hear five young swimmers talking about what's happened to them in the past year. For Questions **19–23**, choose from the list **A–F** what each speaker says. Use the letters only once. There is one extra letter which you do not need to use.

A   I took a break from swimming.

B   I gave up my studies to swim.

C   I went on a swimming tour abroad.

D   I swam for my college team.

E   I had a physical problem.

F   I was a winner of competitions.

Speaker 1 ⬜ **19**

Speaker 2 ⬜ **20**

Speaker 3 ⬜ **21**

Speaker 4 ⬜ **22**

Speaker 5 ⬜ **23**

You will hear an interview with Ricky Foyles, a singer and songwriter. For Questions **24–30**, decide which of the statements are TRUE and which are FALSE and write T for **True** or F for **False** in the boxes provided.

24   Ricky's songs are about the lives of famous people.   ⬜ **24**

25   The message in Ricky's songs is difficult to understand.   ⬜ **25**

26   Ricky's popularity is on the increase.   ⬜ **26**

27   Money is unimportant to Ricky.   ⬜ **27**

28   Ricky has followed the advice of some of his fans.   ⬜ **28**

29   Ricky thinks his fans are disappointed when they meet him.   ⬜ **29**

30   Ricky is anxious about his new album.   ⬜ **30**

Tip Strip

Another task in Part 4 asks you to mark statements true or false.

• Before you listen, underline key words in the statements. Verbs and adjectives are often important.

• Look out for prefixes, e.g. unimportant.

• The ideas in the statements will be mentioned on tape, but does the statement reflect what is said?

Question 25: Ricky says the words in the songs are easy to understand, but what does he say about the message?

Question 27: Ricky talks about his attitude to money in the past and present. Listen for how his attitude has changed.

Question 30: Ricky uses the word 'anxious' when talking about new songs. Does 'anxious' mean worried or not worried?

PAPER 5   Speaking (14 minutes)

Tip Strip

- Listen to the instructions. Make sure you do what is asked.
- Don't be afraid to ask your partner or the examiner to repeat something if you haven't understood.
- Listen to the questions the examiner asks your partner, and listen to what your partner says. The examiner may say 'And what about you?' or 'Do you agree?'.
- Don't give short answers. Say what you think and why.

PART 1   (3 minutes)

The examiner encourages you both to talk briefly about yourselves by answering questions such as:

Do you have any brothers and sisters?
What do the other members of your family do?
Tell us something about the place where you are living at the moment.
What type of house would you like to live in, in the future?

PART 2   (3 or 4 minutes)

You each talk for a minute without interruption in response to a visual prompt. You are encouraged to make a brief comment after your partner has spoken.

People painting (compare, contrast and speculate)

Turn to pictures 1 and 2 on page 154 which show people painting.

Candidate A, compare and contrast these photographs, and say why you think the people are painting. You have a minute to do this.

Candidate B, do you like painting?

People waiting (compare, contrast and speculate)

Turn to pictures 1 and 2 on page 155 which show people waiting in different situations.

Candidate B, compare and contrast these photographs, and say how you think the people are feeling about having to wait. You have a minute to do this.

Candidate A, do you get impatient waiting for things?

PART 3   (3 or 4 minutes)

You both discuss a decision-making / problem-solving task, illustrated by visual material, without interruption by the examiner.

Student advice centre (discuss and evaluate)

Turn to the pictures on page 156 which show ideas for an Advice Centre at an international college for students from abroad.

What kind of advice may students need in each area? Which three areas do you think are the most urgent?

PART 4   (3 or 4 minutes)

The examiner encourages you to develop the discussion in Part 3 by asking questions such as:

Where else might students get advice?
Have you ever asked for advice? When?
Do you think adults should give young people advice even if they don't ask for it?
How difficult is it to follow other people's advice?
How do people in your country feel about spending time abroad on their own?

PAPER 1   Reading (1 hour 15 minutes)

You are going to read an extract from an article about space tourism. Choose from the list **A–H** the sentence which best summarises each part (**1–6**) of the extract. There is one extra sentence which you do not need to use. There is an example at the beginning (**0**).

Mark your answers **on the separate answer sheet**.

A Careers can be planned in readiness for jobs in space tourism.

B We can look forward to a time of widespread space tourism.

C Individuals can contribute in various ways to making space tourism a reality.

D The development of space tourism will depend on the level of commercial investment.

E Financial planning is required now if you want to be a space tourist in the future.

F There are good reasons for encouraging space tourism.

G In its initial phase, space tourism will offer only basic facilities.

H Space tourism is becoming the concern of private companies.

SPACE TOURISM

The idea of what's called Space Tourism, where ordinary members of the public queue up to buy tickets for travel into outer space and back, really stretches the imagination. According to Alan Grant, this distant dream could soon be a reality ...

0	H

On Earth, governments provide a number of services, such as defence, police and a legal system. But most activities are done by individuals and companies and it is going to be the same in space. Over the past few years a growing volume of work has been done on the subject and it is now clear that setting up commercial space tourism services is a realistic target for businesses today.

1	

Many people still think that to get the chance to go to space you have got to try to become an astronaut. Unfortunately, the chances of succeeding are tiny, simply because there are so few astronauts – and there is no prospect of a lot more being employed. However, you need not despair because you will be able to go as a visitor. So for anyone, the first thing you should do if you want to go to space is save up because the demand is expected to be strong and, in the early stages, prices will be high.

2	

In order to stay longer in space, you could work in one of the businesses that will be set up in orbit. There will be opportunities in manufacturing – aerospace vehicle makers, orbital construction, electric power, extra-terrestrial mining, chemical engineering and other fields. So you can start university studies and try to get the sort of work experience that will ensure you are well-placed to apply for a job in any of these areas.

3	

The general public are very interested in travelling to space. Apart from the interest factor, such tourism is the only way in which space activities can become profitable and the quickest way to start to use the limitless resources of space to solve our problems on Earth. And living in space involves every line of business, from construction to marketing, fashion, interior design and law.

4	

It is possible to envisage a future when demand for space tourism travel will grow from thousands of passengers per year to hundreds of thousands per year. Tickets to orbit will cost less and flights will depart from many different airports. Orbital facilities will grow from just being prefabricated modules to large structures constructed for hundreds of guests.

5	

But like any other business, space tourism will develop progressively. Starting as a relatively small-scale and relatively high-priced activity, customers will find that the service will be nearer to 'adventure travel' than to a luxury-style hotel. Orbital accommodation will be safe but rather simple. This will be a time for the pioneers who will not mind the lack of comfort.

6	

Few projects are successfully completed without the help of people who believe in them. It is possible to take an active role in bringing space tourism about by asking airlines, hotels and travel companies if and when they intend to offer space travel. Others may prefer to lend a hand by doing research into one or more of the areas needing it, or by joining one of the many companies that are already working towards a future in space.

You are going to read a magazine article about a young sports person. For Questions **7–14**, choose the correct answer **A**, **B**, **C** or **D**.

Mark your answers **on the separate answer sheet**.

Wakeboarding

Knowing that Tom Finch, a junior champion in the relatively new sport of wakeboarding, had won so many competitions, I was more than a little taken aback to see how slight he was. Wakeboarding, you see, involves being pulled along at high speed behind a power boat, rather like in water skiing, then launching yourself into the air to perform a series of complicated tricks, as in skateboarding or snowboarding. Now, that is a feat you'd think required big bones and bulging muscles. But Tom is just 1.44m tall and weighs 38 kilos.

'It hurt my forearms at first, but now I guess I'm used to it,' Tom told me. At 14 years old, Tom has been practising the sport for just two years, but has already found competing in his age group almost too easy. He didn't say that, of course. Maybe because he didn't want to seem bigheaded, especially with his Dad sitting just a few metres away, or maybe because he just doesn't think it's important. 'I wakeboard because it's fun,' he told me with a smile, 'and scary!'

He knows he's good though and one look at his results confirms that this is justified. Yet when Tom started, the organisers tried to persuade him not to enter his first competition, thinking he'd be upset when he came last. Tom won by a mile and silenced them all. So, what makes him so good? Perhaps putting on a wetsuit, whatever the weather, and practising

for at least two hours everyday. For
42 **that** is what Tom does. He also buys and studies every new wakeboarding video and spends hours working on every new trick, finding new ways to twist and turn his small body.

He's also not afraid to take advice from people better than him. 'I wouldn't be where I am without my trainer,' Tom says. 'It takes so much longer to learn without him; he can spot what I'm doing wrong in a second and put me right. He gives me lots of tips on some of the real technical details too.'

Although the sport is still relatively unknown compared to surfing and snowboarding, which everyone's
59 heard of, Tom reckons it's **on the up**. 'Everyone at school is well aware of it, trying it and loving it,' he says. He's not wrong either. Even on the rainy, windy day that I met him, there's a queue of eager bodies in wetsuits getting into the freezing water at the watersports centre near London where Tom trains.

It will take a few years until the overall standard reaches that of the USA though. Tom told me that everything is twice as fast, twice as big there, which makes it really scary and dangerous. Tom knows no fear though and wants one day to be a professional. He might only be 1.44m tall, but let's not forget that the professionals were all fourteen-year-olds at one time too.

7 What surprised the writer most on first meeting Tom Finch?

    A his height
    B his strength
    C his skilfulness
    D his bravery

8 When asked about his success in competitions, Tom appeared to be

    A embarrassed.
    B proud.
    C modest.
    D nervous.

9 When Tom started entering competitions, people thought

    A he had not been trained.
    B he might hurt himself.
    C he was below the age limit.
    D he would be disappointed.

10 What does 'that' in line 42 refer to?

    A studying hard
    B practising daily
    C buying videos
    D working on new tricks

11 Tom is particularly grateful when his trainer

    A points out his mistakes.
    B makes him work hard.
    C stops him being afraid.
    D spends long hours with him.

12 What does Tom mean by the phrase 'on the up' in line 59?

    A becoming better understood
    B getting more practice
    C getting easier for people
    D becoming more popular

13 In the future, Tom hopes to

    A train others in his sport.
    B go and live in the USA.
    C get over his remaining fears.
    D make the sport his career.

14 In general, what does the writer think of Tom?

    A He's very determined.
    B He's easily persuaded.
    C He's overconfident.
    D He's underachieving.

You are going to read a magazine article about marathon running. Seven sentences have been removed from the article. Choose from the sentences **A–H** the one which fits each gap (**15–20**). There is one extra sentence which you do not need to use. There is an example at the beginning (**0**).

Mark your answers **on the separate answer sheet**.

MARATHON RUNNING – A RECIPE FOR HEALTH?

If ever there was living proof that marathon running keeps you fit, Jenny Wood Allen from Dundee is it. **0** | *H* | She was 71 and she did not even have proper training shoes then.

At first she could only run to the end of her avenue, which is about three quarters of a mile. She had problems getting back and had to either take a bus or ask somebody for a lift. **15**

Scientifically speaking, human beings are perfectly tuned for jumping and running and walking long distances. **16** One of them, Professor Craig Sharp says that if you are reasonably fit, you can probably run for two hours at a medium pace and feel OK. At this point your muscles run out of glycogen – the best source of energy we have.

This means you start using fat for energy, and your body has to work harder to transform fat into energy. This happens at a time when you are starting to feel exhausted. **17** All this is proof – he believes – that the body isn't designed for long-distance running.

Other specialists have a very different opinion. Dr Percy Brown believes that if you train sensibly and prepare several months in advance, it could even help you live longer. **18**

He believes the only problem you may have when running a marathon is exhaustion or a small injury caused by falling or tripping over things. **19** Only 1 in 1,000 actually makes it to hospital.

Another problem may be post-race exhaustion. Surveys show most runners are much more likely to catch colds or develop chest infections in the week after running a race. **20** There is no evidence of lasting disease or an increased risk of illness.

At 87, Jenny Wood Allen will be doing the London marathon for the 13th time this Sunday. And she plans to go on taking part for many years to come.

A He argues that after 16–20 miles, you have to slow down and running gets really hard.

B After a quick top up of water and a rest, most go home and make a full recovery.

C When it comes to marathon running, however, the experts are divided.

D In spite of this, marathon running is bad for your health.

E But this weakening effect on the system is short-lived.

F Within a couple of months, however, she was managing two or three miles.

G This is because running halves your risk of getting heart disease.

H She started by running to the shops, wearing an anorak and carrying her shopping bag.

You are going to read an article about wildlife photographers. For Questions **21–35**, choose from the people (**A–D**). The people may be chosen more than once. There is an example at the beginning (**0**).

Mark your answers **on the separate answer sheet**.

A	George Fenns
B	Paul Sommer
C	Roger Miller
D	Nathan Ribbs

Who

defends a previous employer?	**0**	*D*
learnt to make something at an early age?	**21**	
does not mind working in low temperatures?	**22**	
earned money to buy equipment?	**23**	
needs long preparations before taking photos?	**24**	
completed a university course?	**25**	
likes to photograph what others can't see?	**26**	
would like to work in a milder climate?	**27**	
found his camera gave him confidence?	**28**	
admits his profession may be dangerous?	**29**	
has had something he wrote published?	**30**	
wants to save animals from extinction?	**31**	
turned down a well-paid job?	**32**	
made his own equipment?	**33**	
had an encouraging family?	**34**	
has seen his work used by writers?	**35**	

WILDLIFE PHOTOGRAPHERS

Wildlife photographer **George Fenns** is a man who loves his job. 'When I was three, a neighbour's kid taught me to climb our fence,' he recalls. 'I slipped away and brought back a snake I found on the road. I've been interested in wildlife ever since.' George's parents encouraged his enthusiasm for animals and also nurtured his appreciation of art, which led to photography. 'I sold turtles for two dollars each when I was sixteen,' he says. 'That money got me my first camera.' He now spends three months a year photographing life under water. In 1999 he braved the frigid Pacific Ocean to do a series of photos on salmon, and he also wrote an article about it for a wildlife magazine which won him an award as a journalist. His latest job was in the Arctic in freezing temperatures. 'I'd now like a job where it's warm and sunny,' he says. He never complains about the rigours of his job, but would like to have time to write articles and train young photographers who are starting out in this profession.

Photographer **Paul Sommer** is working in Siberia. 'On bad days it can be minus 20 degrees, with a strong wind,' he says. He protects his film from freezing by keeping it inside his gloves. 'You get used to it,' he says. Siberia is a far cry from his childhood in north Brazil. His years at college gave him no hint of future high adventure either: 'I worked two jobs – as a waiter and as a restaurant manager – to get money for college,' he says. And his efforts paid off when he finished his degree. He was offered a job as a journalist in an award-winning newspaper, but said no to it in order to concentrate on photography. His contract as photographer in Siberia does not pay as much as he would have got as a journalist. However, he has no regrets. 'My photos have been used by researchers who are studying animals here. They have been the basis for important pieces in scientific journals,' he says, 'so this is a very satisfying job.'

Freelance photographer **Roger Miller** is on a contract to take photos of volcanoes, of the lava that flows after an eruption and of the animal life around these areas. He is aware of the risks involved in his assignments, but takes it all in his stride. By age 11 Roger was building his own telescopes and photographing stars. 'I was a very shy kid. The camera made me comfortable around people,' he says. In 1970 a science instructor took Roger and his classmates to Mexico to view a total solar eclipse. It was this experience and the help of the science teacher that prompted him to take up photography as a career. 'My parents wanted me to become a writer,' he says, 'they have not lost hope.' His parents may have to wait a long time because Roger's newest challenge in his next assignment is teaching astronauts how to set up their equipment to photograph the activities around the space vehicle. After that he is planning to take a year off to complete a degree in geology which he started years ago.

Nathan Ribbs spends a lot of his time on a 30-metre-high platform that puts him at eye level with the nests of rare birds in the jungle. The platform is very small and the danger of falling off it is evident to everyone except Roger. 'It's like taking pictures from a hill,' he says. For each of his jobs, the steel structure for the platform often has to go on river canoes and along difficult forest trails. 'But it is very rewarding to see and photograph animals that few people will ever see. I do this work because I think these creatures have to be protected so they won't disappear altogether.' Nathan has no intention of returning to his previous job as a photographer of animals held in captivity. 'Zoos are undergoing very positive changes,' he says, 'they are now a leading method of educating about the natural world. But I've done my share of that kind of photography. This is so much more challenging.'

PART 1   You **must** answer this question.

1   You and a friend participated in your club's Sports Weekend a fortnight ago. Your friend has sent you a letter with a small article from a newspaper about the Sports Weekend. Read the letter and the article, together with the notes. Then write to the newspaper editor saying what your friend suggests and asking them to publish another article.

> *Look at this article in the paper about our Sports Weekend! What they say is not true. I'm going on holiday today. Could you write a letter to the editor using the notes I've made?*

Not true!

sick

rain

The local Milton Club Sports Weekend did not come up to our expectations. The Milton team lost 3 to 1 against Rangers in a match which was very disappointing. The Milton team did not seem to have done enough preparation work and two of its best players simply did not turn up. There were unexplained delays throughout the day and some of the athletics events were cancelled. They will need to do better next year.

3 days a week training!

Write a **letter** of between **120** and **180** words in an appropriate style. Do not write any addresses.

Write an answer to **one** of the Questions **2–5** in this part. Write your answer in **120–180** words in an appropriate style.

2   This is part of a letter from an English friend who will be visiting your country next month.

> *It'll be good to spend a week at your place. Any ideas as to what we might do? Should I bring any special clothes? Do let me know if there is anything I can get you from England.*
>
> *Gary*

Write your **letter**, answering your friend's questions and giving relevant details. Do not write any addresses.

3   You have been asked to write a story for a magazine for young people. Your story must **end** like this:

Clara woke up with a shock. It had been only a dream.

Write your **story**.

4   You have just come back from a two-day study trip to a historic town. Your teacher has asked you to write a report about your visit, saying what you saw during the two days and whether you would recommend a similar visit for other students.

Write your **report**.

5   Answer **one** of the following two questions based on your reading of **one** of the set books.

Either   (**a**) Write a **composition**, describing the good and bad qualities of one of the characters in the book you have read.

Or   (**b**) 'It was very difficult to follow the plot of this story and at times I got lost.' With reference to the book you have read, write a **composition**, saying whether you agree or disagree with this statement and why.

For Questions **1–15**, read the text below and decide which answer **A**, **B**, **C** or **D** best fits each space. There is an example at the beginning (**0**).

Mark your answers **on the separate answer sheet**.

Example:

0 **A** as well as   **B** as long as   **C** as soon as   **D** as good as

0	A	B	C	D
	▭	▭	▭	▭

SINGING FOR A MUSICAL LIFE

According to a group called The Voices Foundation, everyone has a singing voice (**0**) ..... a speaking voice somewhere inside them. This, they say, should be encouraged from an early (**1**) ..... because it provides the best, and the cheapest, (**2**) ..... on which to build an understanding of music.

(**3**) ..... the Foundation's ideas, lies the teaching of the Hungarian composer Zoltan Kodaly. He observed that song can (**4**) ..... a key part of the relationship between mother and child almost from birth. This is especially (**5**) ..... of more traditional societies, like those of West Africa, where some small children are (**6**) ..... to sing literally hundreds of songs, all of which have been learnt by (**7**) ...... But many modern children first (**8**) ..... to an understanding of music when they learn to play an instrument, and (**9**) ..... some teaching of the theory of music is usually a part of this, their relationship with the music on the (**10**) ..... is often a mechanical one.

The (**11**) ..... of the Voices Foundation is that a natural (**12**) ..... for rhythm, harmony and musical structure, the very (**13**) ..... we appreciate in the greatest musicians, can only be achieved through the exploration of music with the voice from the start. The foundation has, therefore, (**14**) ..... itself the task of developing a singing-centred musical education programme that could (**15**) ..... junior pupils all over the world.

1	**A**	start	**B**	life	**C**	time	**D**	age
2	**A**	ground	**B**	basis	**C**	root	**D**	plot
3	**A**	Behind	**B**	Beneath	**C**	Besides	**D**	Between
4	**A**	grow	**B**	do	**C**	form	**D**	make
5	**A**	fact	**B**	true	**C**	real	**D**	actual
6	**A**	able	**B**	expert	**C**	skilled	**D**	fit
7	**A**	repeat	**B**	heart	**C**	memory	**D**	mind
8	**A**	come	**B**	reach	**C**	go	**D**	arrive
9	**A**	however	**B**	despite	**C**	although	**D**	whether
10	**A**	lines	**B**	notes	**C**	book	**D**	page
11	**A**	rule	**B**	certainty	**C**	trust	**D**	belief
12	**A**	awareness	**B**	touch	**C**	grasp	**D**	feeling
13	**A**	degrees	**B**	qualities	**C**	measures	**D**	practices
14	**A**	let	**B**	set	**C**	put	**D**	cut
15	**A**	benefit	**B**	favour	**C**	gain	**D**	profit

For Questions **16–30**, read the text below and think of the word which best fits each space. Use only **one** word in each space. There is an example at the beginning (**0**).

Write your answers **on the separate answer sheet**.

Example:	**0**	*was*

THE BIRTH OF THE T-SHIRT

The T-shirt, or at least the T-shirt as we know it, (**0**) .... born in the theatre. When Tennessee William's play *A Streetcar Named Desire* opened in New York in December 1947, a young actor (**16**) .... Marlon Brando went (**17**) .... stage wearing a (**18**) .... of blue jeans and a bright, white, capped-sleeve T-shirt. It was the first time the T-shirt (**19**) .... been seen publicly as anything (**20**) .... an item of underwear and it set a fashion trend that was to last through (**21**) .... the end of the century.

The idea for the T-shirt came (**22**) .... Brando himself. He had worn one at rehearsals for the play. The director was (**23**) .... impressed by the look that was created that he asked Brando to wear the shirt in the play itself. Brando may have seen the shirt being advertised by the American company Sears Roebuck. They had decided to market the shirt (**24**) .... a fashionable garment in its (**25**) .... right, rather than just something to be worn (**26**) .... warmth beneath a denim workshirt (**27**) .... an army uniform.

It was Brando, however, (**28**) .... popularised it, especially with (**29**) .... release of the film version of *Streetcar* in 1951. A short leather jacket completed the look that was to be adopted (**30**) .... teenage rebels in many countries for decades afterwards.

For Questions **31–40**, complete the second sentence so that it has a similar meaning to the first sentence, using the word given. **Do not change the word given.** You must use between two and five words, including the word given. Here is an example (**0**).

Example: **0**   It was the most relaxing holiday I ever had.

　　　　　　such

　　　　　　I have never .... holiday.

The gap can be filled by the words 'had such a relaxing' so you write:

0	had such a relaxing

Write **only the missing words** on the separate answer sheet.

---

31   I find Robert's taste in music very hard to tolerate.

　　put

　　I find it hard .... Robert's taste in music.

32   I find waiting for buses very boring.

　　get

　　I find .... waiting for buses.

33   It's very difficult to predict the weather here.

　　tends

　　The weather .... unpredictable here.

34   People say learning lists of words is not a good use of time.

　　waste

　　Learning lists of words is .... of time.

35   Christine complained formally when her course of study was cancelled.

　　made

　　Christine .... when her course of study was cancelled.

36   'I find all the advertisements on TV really irritating,' said John.

　　nerves

　　'All the advertisements on TV really ....,' said John.

37   Mark regretted selling his old motorbike.

　　wished

　　Mark .... his old motorbike.

38   'If you take my advice, Paul,' said Lynda, 'you should buy a personal computer.'

　　advised

　　Lynda .... a personal computer.

39   Pauline hadn't expected to see so many people at the concert.

　　surprise

　　It came .... to see so many people at the concert.

40   Golf is becoming increasingly popular in Britain.

　　popularity

　　The .... in Britain.

For Questions **41–55**, read the text below and look carefully at each line. Some of the lines are correct, and some have a word which should not be there.

If a line is correct, put a tick (✔) by the number **on the separate answer sheet**. If a line has a word which should not be there, write the word **on the separate answer sheet**. There are examples at the beginning (**0** and **00**).

Examples:	**0**	*in*
	00	✔

TV CRITIC

0 .... I am replying to the letter which you published in last week from

00 .... a girl called Jessica on the subject of television. I am not what you

41 .... would call a television addict, and I am agree that there are badly-

42 .... written programmes which they contain unnecessary bad language

43 .... and violence, but television does have its good points. Many of the

44 .... programmes which are broadcast on are educational and can help

45 .... with schoolwork. A good soap-opera or comedy it is a source of

46 .... the relaxation for many people. Television also provides jobs

47 .... for thousands of people, so that think how much unemployment there

48 .... would be without it. In general, therefore, I think that television is

49 .... a good thing. There is, however, one most thing I would like to

50 .... complain about, and that there is the amount of smoking in the films

51 .... that are shown on television. Adults are always lecturing up children

52 .... about how they shouldn't to smoke, and yet we see many smoking

53 .... scenes on television. What's more so, smoking is often shown as a

54 .... very 'cool' thing to do, making young people much more likely to

55 .... copy what they see and take up with smoking themselves.

For Questions **56–65**, read the text below. Use the word given in capitals at the end of each line to form a word that fits in the space in the same line. There is an example at the beginning (**0**). Write your answers **on the separate answer sheet**.

Example: | **0** | *happiness*

HAPPY IS HEALTHY

Medical research has found that (**0**) .*happiness*. has a strongly   **HAPPY**
beneficial effect on health. The healing properties of (**56**) .... are   **LAUGH**
such that humour is now being used alongside more (**57**) ....   **TRADITION**
courses of (**58**) .... in some hospitals. In a London children's   **TREAT**
hospital, for example, two clowns are provided for the (**59**) .... of   **ENTERTAIN**
patients. Doctors say that these clowns are (**60**) .... in making the   **SUCCESS**
children feel better.

It seems that when we laugh, there can be a (**61**) .... in both   **REDUCE**
blood pressure and the amount of (**62**) .... in our muscles.   **TENSE**
Although it is (**63**) .... to prove it at the moment, this may also   **POSSIBLE**
mean that people who feel unhappy and who are, therefore,
(**64**) .... to laugh so much, suffer more often from physical   **LIKELY**
(**65**) ....   **ILL**

PAPER 4

Listening (40 minutes)

You will hear people talking in eight different situations. For Questions **1–8**, choose the best answer **A**, **B** or **C**.

1 On the radio you hear an announcement about a future programme. What type of programme is being discussed?

   A   a play
   B   an interview
   C   a music programme

                                                                             1

2 You hear a School Principal talking on the phone. Who is he talking to?

   A   a teacher
   B   an architect
   C   a secretary

   2

3 You hear a scientist talking about pollution on the radio. What do scientists need to know more about?

   A   the animals at risk
   B   the causes of the problem
   C   the effects on plants

   3

4 You hear part of a play about life in a school. Who is talking?

   A   one of the teachers
   B   the Head Teacher
   C   one of the students

   4

5 You hear a man talking about his tent. What does he like about it?

   A   It is easy to put up.
   B   It is large.
   C   It is waterproof.

   5

6 You hear part of nature programme on the radio. Why are kangaroos being studied?

   A   to help protect their environment
   B   to learn about fitness from them
   C   to make sure they are in good health

   6

7 You hear the weather forecast on the radio. What will the weather be like tomorrow afternoon?

   A   cloudier than in the morning
   B   warmer than in the morning
   C   windier than in the morning

   7

8 You hear a news report about a fire. Where did the fire take place?

   A   in a food storage area
   B   in a restaurant
   C   in agricultural buildings

   8

You will hear an archaeologist talking about her job. For Questions **9–18**, complete the sentences.

Anna first thought she'd like to be an archaeologist after she saw a

	9

Anna prefers archaeology to history because it is a [   ] **10** activity.

Recently Anna and her colleagues found a [   ] **11** in London.

Much of Anna's time is spent dealing with the [   ] **12** produced by other archaeologists.

One of Anna's responsibilities is to check that the

and	**13**

of the excavation are in the right place.

After cleaning the piece she has found, Anna has to [   ] **14** it.

Anna finds it interesting to clean an old wall because she may learn

and	**15**

it was built.

Anna particularly dislikes working in [   ] **16** because they're hot and dusty.

Archaeologists use scientific techniques to find out about the

	17

of people in past centuries.

The Archaeology Service is often involved in helping

	18

to understand the law.

PART 3

You will hear five people saying why they became professional artists. For Questions **19–23**, choose from the list **A–F** what each speaker says. Use the letters only once. There is one extra letter which you do not need to use.

Why I became a professional artist

A   I needed to earn a living.

B   I had relatives who gave me support.

C   I did not have other skills.

D   I was offered an interesting job.

E   I wanted to avoid academic studies.

F   I was persuaded by somebody else.

Speaker 1 [ ] **19**

Speaker 2 [ ] **20**

Speaker 3 [ ] **21**

Speaker 4 [ ] **22**

Speaker 5 [ ] **23**

PART 4

You will hear a conversation about three films, *Imitation*, *Midday Train*, and *Postman Gregg*. For Questions **24–30**, decide which of the following is said about each film. Write **I** for *Imitation*, **M** for *Midday Train* or **P** for *Postman Gregg*.

24   This film deals with unattractive characters. [ ] **24**

25   This film has some very good actors. [ ] **25**

26   This film is based on real-life events. [ ] **26**

27   This film ends in an unexpected way. [ ] **27**

28   This film has a plot that is difficult to follow. [ ] **28**

29   This film is about travelling adventures. [ ] **29**

30   This film shows interesting scenery. [ ] **30**

Tip Strip

Another task in Part 4 asks you to match statements to three different speakers or topics.
- Before you listen, underline the key words in the questions. Adjectives and nouns are often important.
- The films will be discussed altogether. Listen out for pronouns such as *it*, *that one*, *the other one*, etc. Which films do they refer to?

Question 24: The woman describes the characters in one film as 'unpleasant'. But which film is she talking about?

Question 30: This question talks about scenery. One of the films takes place mostly indoors, another doesn't show much of the countries it's based in. So which is the film with the wonderful views of hills, lakes, etc.?

PAPER 5

Speaking (14 minutes)

PART 1 (3 minutes)

Answer these questions:

Do you work or do you study?
Can you tell us something about the place where you study or work?
What type of work would you like to do in the future?
What qualifications do you think you'll need in the future?

PART 2 (3 or 4 minutes)

Working at home (compare, contrast and speculate)

Turn to pictures 1 and 2 on page 157 which show people who work at home.

Candidate A, compare and contrast these photographs, and say why you think the people have chosen to work at home. You have a minute to do this.

Candidate B, would you like to work at home?

On holiday (compare, contrast and speculate)

Turn to pictures 1 and 2 on page 158 which show people on holiday.

Candidate B, compare and contrast these photographs, and say why you think the people have chosen this type of holiday. You have a minute to do this.

Candidate A, do you like city holidays?

PART 3 (3 or 4 minutes)

Youth centre (discuss and evaluate)

Turn to the pictures on page 159 which show ideas for a Youth centre. A local council has got an old house they want to use for the centre. Look at the plan of the house and the suggestions for how each area could be used.

How popular would the various suggestions be with young people? How would you use the space available?

PART 4 (3 or 4 minutes)

Answer these questions:

Which of the activities would you choose to do in a Youth centre? Why?
How necessary is it to have spaces for young people only?
Which age groups do you think should be admitted to a Youth centre?
What spaces do young people have in your country?
How easy is it for young people to get on with older people?
Do you think life for young people is easier or more difficult than it was in the past?

TEST 4

PART 1   You are going to read an article about an island off the coast of south-west England. Choose the most suitable heading from the list **A–I** for each part (**1–7**) of the article. There is one extra heading which you do not need to use. There is an example at the beginning (**0**).

Mark your answers **on the separate answer sheet**.

A	A natural fortress	**D**	A lack of variety	**G**	A surprising impression
B	An unfortunate choice	**E**	A chance to escape	**H**	An unexpected development
C	An undeserved reputation	**F**	A range of facilities	**I**	A mystery solved

Across to Lundy Island

Andrew Osmond took a boat to Lundy – an island where the weather is no laughing matter

0   *I*

I had always been slightly puzzled as to why the boat trip to Lundy Island, eleven miles off the coast of Devon in south-west England, takes such a long time. The scheduled two-hour journey time seems excessive. Now, three hours into the voyage, the island felt no nearer than when I had boarded the ship. I began to understand something of Lundy's isolation, for this stretch of water, where the Atlantic Ocean meets the Bristol Channel can be very rough.

 1

The captain's voice came over the loudspeaker, 'Would all day visitors please report to the main lounge area.' It was the only thing to make me smile during the whole voyage; the shocked expression on the faces of the day-trippers as they realised they'd have to spend the night on the island because the sea was too rough for the return crossing. Those of us who had pre-booked accommodation on the island could afford to look smug.

 2

My thoughts were already turning to the warm little stone house that was awaiting my arrival on dry land. And suddenly, we were there. Lundy presents a formidable face to seaborne arrivals. Its cliffs rise 400 feet, along the island's three-mile length, and fingers of rock jut out into the sea, making the water dance white with agitation. It is not surprising that the island has resisted all attempts at invasion over the centuries.

 3

The tiny collection of stone buildings that make up the village of Lundy are situated at the southern end of the island, and here you find the only anchorage too. The clear blue water of the landing bay made me think we must have taken a wrong turn at sea and somehow found ourselves coming ashore on one of the Greek Islands. I had never seen such beautiful waters around the English coast.

 4

Before leaving home, I had read that Lundy was famous for its diving and snorkelling, but I had laughed at the idea of swimming in these cold seas and had left my snorkel and face mask behind. Now, confronted with this brilliant-blue truth, I was almost beginning to regret my decision. I would certainly come to regret leaving behind my hooded waterproof jacket and my torch, in favour of a smart shirt for the evenings that was clearly not needed.

 5

The absence of any true native population on Lundy means that as a tourist, you don't feel that you are invading anyone's privacy. Most of the residents are people employed to look after the welfare of visitors. The rental accommodation is both imaginative and evocative of the island's past. There are 166 buildings for rent. You can choose between a 12-room castle, a fisherman's cottage or, like me, a modest lighthouse keeper's house.

 6

When I told people that I was going to Lundy, the most frequent remarks were, 'Won't you be bored and lonely?' and 'Isn't it only for bird-watchers?' What surprised me on arrival was just how diverse a range of activities my fellow travellers were planning. As well as divers, there were rock-climbers, artists, naturalists and, of course, some birdwatchers because Lundy is deservedly famous as a haven for all kinds of seabirds.

 7

But, should you be thinking of a trip to Lundy, remember that you don't have to take part in the outdoor pursuits. The most popular activity on Lundy these days must be doing very little. I went for rest and relaxation and found it in abundance. I suggest taking a good book and then finding a sheltered corner where you can enjoy the beautiful scenery and the incomparable tranquillity.

PART 2

You are going to read a magazine article about a young mother whose house was burgled. For Questions **8–15**, choose the correct answer **A**, **B**, **C** or **D**.

Mark your answers **on the separate answer sheet**.

Lisa Tyler was weary after a long, hard day at the pottery factory where she works. But as she approached her home in the English city of Stoke-on-Trent, her heart lightened; soon she would be having a nice cup of tea, putting her feet up and watching *Friends*, her favourite TV series.
5 But first, she needed to change out of her work clothes and **pick up** her three-year-old son from his grandmother's house nearby.

As Lisa walked up her garden path, she noticed a light flashing on and off in an upstairs bedroom. A shiver went down her back. What if it was a burglar? Quietly, she crept round to the back of the house to see if there was any sign of a break-in. Sure enough, a window was open and someone's coat was hanging on the gatepost!

Well, 26-year-old Lisa didn't fancy coming face to face with a burglar, so she ran to a neighbour's house and rang the police. But as she sat waiting for the police to arrive, Lisa's curiosity got the better of her and she decided to go back and see what was going on. That's when she saw a leg coming out of the downstairs front window. It was a man climbing out. Lisa gasped in shock. The burglar was carrying her portable television!

18 At this point, **Lisa saw red**. She didn't have many possessions and she'd saved long and hard to buy that set. Besides, nobody was going to stop her watching *Friends*.

'Oh no you don't,' she muttered under her breath, as the fury swelled inside her. Without even stopping to think, she tore across the garden and started shouting at the burglar. 'Give me my TV – drop it now!' she screamed.

Ignoring her, the man fled across the garden. So Lisa threw herself at him and successfully rugby-tackled him to the ground. The burglar struggled to escape, but Lisa hung on like the best kind of guard dog despite being punched and kicked. As she looked up, she realised that she recognised the burglar's face. She was so surprised that she lost her grip and the burglar got away, leaving the TV behind in the garden.

By the time the police and her father arrived, Lisa was in tears. 'I can't believe you were so foolish, Lisa,' scolded her father. 'You could have been killed.'

'I know, but at least he didn't get my TV,' she replied.

Lisa later remembered the name of the burglar, who had been in the same year as her at school. He was later caught and jailed for 15 months after admitting burglary and assault. In May last year, Lisa was given a Certificate of Appreciation by Staffordshire Police, for her 'outstanding courage and public action'. But in the future she intends to leave household security to a new member of her family, Chan, who is a real guard dog.

8 How was Lisa feeling as she walked home from work?

    A tired
    B anxious
    C depressed
    D relieved

9 What does 'pick up' mean in line 5?

    A contact
    B visit
    C collect
    D check

10 What first led Lisa to think there was a burglar in her house?

    A Something had been broken.
    B Something had been left outside.
    C Something was in the wrong place.
    D Something was moving inside.

11 Why didn't Lisa wait in her neighbour's house until the police arrived?

    A She was worried about losing her television.
    B She wanted to know what was happening.
    C She noticed something from her neighbour's window.
    D She realised that the burglar was leaving.

12 What does 'Lisa saw red' (line 18) mean?

    A She got impatient.
    B She felt frightened.
    C She got angry.
    D She felt brave.

13 What happened when Lisa shouted at the burglar?

    A He tried to explain why he was there.
    B He fell over as he ran towards her.
    C He pretended not to have heard her.
    D He dropped the TV and attacked her.

14 What did Lisa's father do when he arrived?

    A He told her off.
    B Her comforted her.
    C He praised her.
    D He argued with her.

15 How was the burglar caught?

    A Lisa was able to describe him.
    B He was found at another burglary.
    C Lisa realised she could identify him.
    D He was already known to the police.

You are going to read a magazine article about herons. Seven sentences have been removed from the article. Choose from the sentences **A–H** the one which fits each gap (**16–21**). There is one extra sentence which you do not need to use. There is an example at the beginning (**0**).

Mark your answers **on the separate answer sheet**.

HERONS

Herons are beautiful birds. Years ago, as I walked to work in a fish factory in Aberdeen, herons would always bring a little bit of light to the dark winter mornings. Usually there would be a couple of them standing on the river's edge. | **0** | *H* |

This natural cautiousness is usual in herons. They prefer to spend the day in areas where they can hunt for fish in peace. They seldom allow close approach and are quick to take to the air when they sense humans are about. | **16** | |

This cruel treatment is now on the decline and consequently the latest *Bird Atlas* estimates there are probably twice as many herons breeding in Britain today than in the late 1960s. | **17** | | This means herons can feed and survive in areas which were previously unavailable because they were either too cold or ruined by poisonous substances in the water.

Weather is probably the single most important factor in the improvement in the heron population. In effect, new areas of habitat have been opened up. | **18** | | The one of 1963 had a notable impact, but surprisingly there is little to suggest that the same happened in the freezing temperatures of 1979 and 1892.

| **19** | | As well as the UK, similar increases have been recorded throughout Europe. By the early 1970s, the heron had become threatened in many parts of central Europe, but has since recovered dramatically. And if not persecuted, will even breed in city centres, such as happens in Amsterdam.

| **20** | | There are still numerous threats, mostly to do with habitat degradation, and which certainly affect populations on a local scale. Drainage of fields and excavation reduce food supplies. The planting of forests, while providing nesting sites, may also reduce the water flow in some water courses and hence fish availability.

The heron lives on fish. | **21** | | On other occasions a different tactic is adopted, this time slowly stalking through the water, looking intently at any stirrings. If the need arises, the heron will wade deep until the body is afloat and it can even swim for a short distance. They are such a delight to watch, particularly in the morning when they go hunting in the frost-draped winter semi-darkness.

A Another reason for this increase can be found in the milder winters and the reduction in water pollution.

B Further north the bird is equally widespread, although it is absent from areas of high ground.

C Such nervousness is understandable, given that they have suffered from persecution from fish farmers.

D While heron numbers have increased, it is important not to be complacent.

E However, a hard winter will temporarily set numbers back.

F The commonest hunting technique is to stand still by the water's edge, with only the eyes twinkling as it carefully scans for fish.

G It appears, however, that all is well for the heron at the moment.

H But once dawn broke, the herons would move upstream to quieter stretches of the river.

You are going to read a magazine article about holidays abroad. For Questions **22–35**, choose from the people (**A–D**). The people may be chosen more than once. There is an example at the beginning (**0**).

Mark your answers **on the separate answer sheet**.

A	**Graham Buckley**
B	**Tom Farley**
C	**Peter Sampson**
D	**Gordon Monts**

Which of the people A–D

goes to a different place each time?	**0**	*D*
finds some written information inadequate?	**22**	
is careful to keep his money safe?	**23**	
is dissatisfied with airport staff?	**24**	
prefers to take little equipment with him?	**25**	
gives advice on travel documents?	**26**	
believes he ruined somebody else's holiday?	**27**	
had a problem at an airport?	**28**	
thinks travellers should do some reading?	**29**	
is nervous before trips?	**30**	
informs travel agents about his walking skills?	**31**	
shows respect for local cultures?	**32**	
finds communicating in the local language helpful?	**33**	
asks mountain climbers for advice?	**34**	
is careless with his luggage?	**35**	

Graham Buckley has been climbing hills ever since he was eight. He books his walking holidays through travel agents. He believes there is plenty of choice when it comes to deciding where to go, with something to match everyone's abilities and aspirations. 'But matching your ability with what you find in a brochure isn't easy,' he says. 'What you find is an attractive description but the brochure won't give you a breakdown of the skills required.' His advice is to get information about the chosen area from the abundant printed material available, before starting off. 'It should not be forgotten that once you are in a foreign country, you may have trouble finding out information if your command of the language is shaky.' Graham is convinced that people usually pack last minute and as a result take too much gear. 'I find it's virtually impossible to take too little equipment,' he says, 'unless you forget to take your boots and passport, of course!'

Tom Farley likes to play safe when he books his walking holidays ever since he found himself struggling up a steep mountain that he was ill-prepared for. 'What I regret most about it is that I ruined the walking experience for the others because they had to keep waiting for me,' he says. He now asks the travel agents about the area he'll be covering and gives them details about the type of walking he normally does to allow them to match his ability to a suitable walking holiday. Tom is also very careful when it comes to packing his rucksack. 'If I am flying, I put the rucksack inside a large bag with a zip,' he says, 'the people who handle luggage at airports are often very careless and things could go very wrong if you find your rucksack's damaged.' What Tom likes best about his travelling experiences is the chance to use the languages he has learnt. 'Just a few words of the local language make all the difference to a trip,' he says. 'People will help you

TRICKS OF THE TRADE

Walking in a foreign country

If you're planning to go on your first walking holiday abroad, make sure it runs smoothly … Alan Barns gives us the opinions of four experienced travellers.

solve any problems you may have if you try and speak their language.'

Peter Sampson is also a seasoned traveller and believes that in order to enjoy a walking holiday abroad it is important to get the essential things right. 'Your trip of a lifetime could easily get off to a slow start if you don't arrive in time for the flight,' he says. 'Arriving just in time is risky, I did it once and found that someone else had already taken my seat.' No less important, he says, is working out a plan to carry your cash safely. 'It is not a good idea to just stuff it in your pocket,' he says. Peter usually gets on very well with the local inhabitants and makes an effort to respect their customs. 'Every country has its unique rules that local people live by,' he says, 'and you can appear rude if you, for example, wear the wrong sort of clothes. I don't speak any foreign languages, but I ask local people who speak English for advice in this respect.'

Gordon Monts goes on a mountain climbing holiday twice a year, and has so far never been to the same place twice. In spite of his experience, he admits to feeling uneasy when preparing for a trip. 'I've never had anything go wrong, but I know things can happen, and do happen.' Just in case things do go wrong, Gordon thinks it is a good idea to keep a record of his passport number and flight numbers, and makes copies of all the holiday papers the travel agent gives him. 'This is a good idea, particularly if you are as bad as I am at looking after your rucksack and things.' Once at his destination, he spends a day or two studying the mountain routes he has chosen. 'Even if you have done a lot of preparation beforehand, you need to look at your plan again. There are usually many other people who have already climbed in the area, so I talk to them and get lots of good tips.'

PART 1

You **must** answer this question.

1   You are planning to do an English course in an English-speaking country with a friend who has sent you a letter with an advertisement. Read the letter and the advertisement together with the notes. Then write to the Seymour Travel Agency asking for the information which your friend suggests and adding any relevant questions of your own.

I found this advertisement and thought they sounded serious and well-organised. I'm going to see my grandparents for a few days, so could you write to them asking for more details? I have made a few notes and maybe you can think of other points.

Thanks. See you soon.

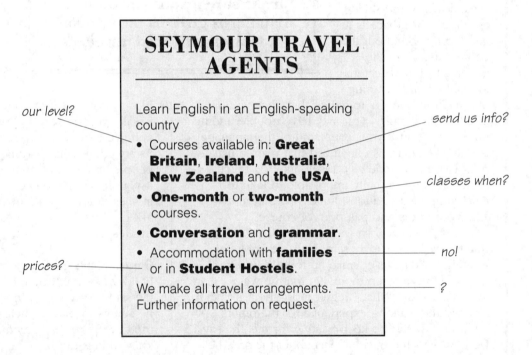

SEYMOUR TRAVEL AGENTS

our level?

send us info?

Learn English in an English-speaking country

- Courses available in: **Great Britain**, **Ireland**, **Australia**, **New Zealand** and **the USA**.

- **One-month** or **two-month** courses.

classes when?

- **Conversation** and **grammar**.

- Accommodation with **families** or in **Student Hostels**.

prices?

no!

We make all travel arrangements. Further information on request.

?

Write a **letter** of between **120** and **180** words in an appropriate style. Do not write any addresses.

Write an answer to **one** of the Questions **2–5** in this part. Write your answer in **120–180** words in an appropriate style.

2   This is part of a letter you received from an English friend:

> When I saw you last summer you said you were going to join the new sports club in your area. How often do you go? What sports can you do? Do they organise competitions? Have you made any new friends there?
>
> Please write soon,
>
> Jack

Write your **letter**, answering Jack's questions and giving relevant details. Do not write any addresses.

3   Your teacher has asked you to write a story for the school magazine. The story must begin like this:

Anna was walking home when the storm broke out. Where could she find shelter? There was a house only 50 metres away.

Write your **story**.

4   An international magazine has asked you to write an article describing your home town and saying what attractions it has for young visitors.

Write your **article**.

5   Answer **one** of the following two questions based on your reading of **one** of the set books.

Either (a) Which part of the story you read did you like the least? Write a **composition**, describing the part you liked least and explaining why.

Or (b) 'One of the characters in the story I have read is uninteresting and boring.' With reference to the book you have read, write a **composition**, saying whether you agree or disagree with this statement and why.

Use of English (1 hour 15 minutes)

For Questions **1–15**, read the text below and decide which answer **A**, **B**, **C** or **D** best fits each space. There is an example at the beginning (**0**).

Mark your answers **on the separate answer sheet**.

Example:

0	**A** answer	**B** reason	**C** explanation	**D** solution

0	**A** ▭	**B** ▯	**C** ▯	**D** ▯

WHALES

How far would you travel for a good meal? If you were a humpback whale, the (**0**) ..... would be five thousand miles. These large sea animals travel at least that far from their winter home off the (**1**) ..... of Columbia to their summer (**2**) ..... areas off Antarctica. The distance covered by some types of whale is amazing, especially when you (**3**) ..... their enormous size. The blue whale is the largest animal that has ever (**4**) ..... and it can weigh as much as thirty elephants. It (**5**) ..... as no surprise, therefore, to hear that ancient folk legends tell of sailors (**6**) ..... these creatures for islands.

The more we (**7**) ..... about whales, the more wonderful they seem. Some species can (**8**) ..... their breath for more than an hour and dive to a (**9**) ..... of over 2000 metres. They use a system of sounds (**10**) ..... as echo-location to find the fish they eat and they have further sounds to keep in (**11**) ..... with each other. The noises they (**12**) ..... can travel hundreds of miles under water. Some species seem to sing complicated songs which (**13**) ..... of a number of separate themes, sung in a specific order which can (**14**) ..... up to half an hour or more. If you ever get the (**15**) ..... to see one of these great creatures in the wild, you will understand why they have inspired so many legends.

1	**A** beach	**B** coast	**C** seaside	**D** ground
2	**A** feeding	**B** dining	**C** eating	**D** chewing
3	**A** view	**B** think	**C** consider	**D** believe
4	**A** been	**B** stayed	**C** born	**D** lived
5	**A** gets	**B** comes	**C** goes	**D** seems
6	**A** supposing	**B** mixing	**C** confusing	**D** mistaking
7	**A** find out	**B** look out	**C** show up	**D** turn up
8	**A** store	**B** keep	**C** hold	**D** save
9	**A** depth	**B** length	**C** width	**D** breadth
10	**A** called	**B** known	**C** referred	**D** named
11	**A** reach	**B** touch	**C** call	**D** range
12	**A** provide	**B** propose	**C** process	**D** produce
13	**A** consist	**B** compose	**C** include	**D** involve
14	**A** long	**B** last	**C** play	**D** give
15	**A** break	**B** choice	**C** chance	**D** luck

For Questions **16–30**, read the text below and think of the word which best fits each space. Use only **one** word in each space. There is an example at the beginning (**0**).

Write your answers **on the separate answer sheet**.

Example: | **0** | *how* |

A PIANO AROUND THE HOUSE

Have you ever asked yourself (**0**) .... people passed the long evenings in the days before television? The answer is that those (**16**) .... could afford it used to play the piano, or (**17**) .... the very least tried to persuade their daughters to (**18**) .... so. Although there is less piano-playing nowadays, pianos are still (**19**) .... interest to collectors of antiques, both as instruments and as pieces of furniture.

As a result, it is once (**20**) .... very fashionable, amongst those (**21**) .... both money and space, to have a grand piano in the living room. Not (**22**) .... pianos, however, are equally fashionable. It would be a mistake to (**23**) .... too excited about the possible resale value of a modern piano bought ten years (**24**) ...., for example. Similarly, not every old piano is going to be a good investment.

Rather (**25**) .... television sets today, they were made (**26**) .... huge numbers in the early twentieth century. At that time, pianos became (**27**) .... popular that most sizeable towns had a local manufacturer. Newly-married couples frequently got (**28**) .... as a main wedding present. So nowadays, many pianos are (**29**) .... little more than the value of the materials they are made from, and end their days being chopped (**30**) .... for firewood.

For Questions **31–40**, complete the second sentence so that it has a similar meaning to the first sentence, using the word given. **Do not change the word given.** You must use between two and five words, including the word given. Here is an example (**0**).

Example: **0**   It is said that gardening is very good exercise.

            supposed

            Gardening .... very good exercise.

The gap can be filled by the words 'is supposed to be' so you write:

0	is supposed to be

Write **only the missing words** on the separate answer sheet.

---

31   The new one-way system seems pointless to me.

    point

    I can't .... the new one-way system.

32   The old house will need a thorough redecoration before you can live in it.

    have

    The old house .... redecorated before you can live in it.

33   Unless you promise to get back in time for lunch, you can't borrow the car.

    long

    You can borrow the car .... to be back in time for lunch.

34   Paula never succeeded in getting her homework done on time.

    able

    Paula was .... her homework done on time.

35   Carrie doesn't run as fast as Sarah.

    runner

    Sarah is .... than Carrie.

36   It was necessary to follow the instructions exactly.

    had

    The instructions .... exactly.

37   It may be dark when you get back, so take a torch with you.

    case

    Take a torch with you .... dark when you get back.

38   This old car probably won't last for more than a year.

    unlikely

    This old car .... for more than one year.

39   It isn't easy for Daniel to get up before the sun rises.

    difficulty

    Daniel .... up before the sun rises.

40   David remembered to take everything except his front door key.

    forgot

    The only thing which .... his front door key.

For Questions **41–55**, read the text below and look carefully at each line. Some of the lines are correct, and some have a word which should not be there.

If a line is correct, put a tick (✔) by the number **on the separate answer sheet**. If a line has a word which should not be there, write the word **on the separate answer sheet**. There are examples at the beginning (**0** and **00**).

Examples:	0	*whose*
	00	✔

HOW TO BE ANIMAL FRIENDLY

0	....	I am writing to recommend a book whose called 'How to be Animal
00	....	Friendly', which I read recently. This is a book for young people
41	....	who are interested in animals but don't know how much about them.
42	....	It has great cartoons and photographs and is packed with them facts
43	....	about the relationship between people and animals. There are written
44	....	chapters on vegetarianism, wearing fur and leather and endangered
45	....	animals. It is written in such a way that it helps you for to see things
46	....	from the animals' viewpoint. In some of places, this book was
47	....	so much sad that I wanted to cry, but on the whole it is fun to read.
48	....	As well as facts about the animals mostly themselves, there is also
49	....	information about that what cruel people do to animals, and how
50	....	people use animals for different things in various parts of the world.
51	....	It also tells you how animals have been saved people's lives. For example,
52	....	I was amazed to read the such exciting story of how three wild bears
53	....	saved a five-year-old girl when she got lost in the woods. I thought
54	....	this book was excellent and would definitely recommend it as for anyone
55	....	over the seven years old who wants to know more about animals.

For Questions **56–65**, read the text below. Use the word given in capitals at the end of each line to form a word that fits in the space in the same line. There is an example at the beginning (**0**). Write your answers **on the separate answer sheet**.

Example: | **0** | *punctuality*

ON TIME

For many people, (**0**) .*punctuality*. is a big issue. Parents are often   **PUNCTUAL**
keen to impress upon their children the (**56**) .... of being   **IMPORTANT**
punctual because they see it as an aspect of (**57**) .... and   **POLITE**
consideration for others. It is also a quality that (**58**) ....   **EMPLOY**
regard as very positive, and those who are (**59**) .... unpunctual   **USUAL**
may end up being (**60**) .... in their careers as a result.   **SUCCESS**

It may be, however, that less punctual people have (**61**) ....   **CHOOSE**
a more (**62**) .... lifestyle than those who always arrive on time.   **RELAX**
They may find it (**63**) .... when so much emphasis is placed   **STRESS**
on timekeeping. Indeed, if others get (**64**) .... when   **PATIENCE**
they are late for appointments, this may not seem (**65**) ....   **REASON**
to them.

PAPER 4

Listening (40 minutes)

You will hear people talking in eight different situations. For Questions **1–8**, choose the best answer **A**, **B** or **C**.

1 You hear an announcement on the radio about a competition.
   In the competition, what do you have to answer a question about?
   A a film
   B wildlife
   C clothing

   [ ] **1**

2 You hear an announcement on the radio.
   What problem does the radio station have this morning?
   A lack of information
   B lack of staff
   C lack of time

   [ ] **2**

3 You hear an advertisement on the radio.
   What is being advertised?
   A an article of clothing
   B a type of bag
   C a piece of electronic equipment

   [ ] **3**

4 You hear a man talking about a sub-tropical island.
   How does he feel about the island?
   A It should become a centre for research.
   B There should be no human activity at all.
   C It should be developed as a tourist resort.

   [ ] **4**

5 You hear a woman talking about a rock music festival.
   What does she like about the festival?
   A the organisation
   B the performances
   C the atmosphere

   [ ] **5**

6 You hear a news report about an outdoor market.
   What is the advantage of the market to customers?
   A The food costs less than elsewhere.
   B There is more information about the food.
   C There is a wider variety of food.

   [ ] **6**

7 You hear a woman talking about an experience while travelling in Africa. In her opinion, why did the hippopotamus go away?
   A It lost interest in them.
   B It was hurt by one of the oars.
   C It was frightened by the noise.

   [ ] **7**

8 You hear somebody complaining about plans to open a restaurant.
   What does he say?
   A The food will be unhealthy.
   B The streets will be dangerous.
   C The local shops will be affected.

   [ ] **8**

You will hear an interview with a man who plays the traditional Australian musical instrument called the didgeridoo. For Questions **9–18**, complete the sentences.

Today's celebration of the didgeridoo is being held at a

| **9** | in England.

Didgeridoos are made from wood that has been attacked by

| **10** |

After making the instrument, the aborigine people use

| **11** | to put traditional artwork on it.

Bob is keen to correct the interviewer when she describes him as an

| **12** |

Bob was first attracted to the | **13** | of the didgeridoo.

The earliest evidence of the didgeridoo comes from pictures found in

| **14** | in Australia.

Didgeridoos are believed to have existed as long as | **15** | years ago.

When playing the didgeridoo, it's important not to | **16** |

To keep a note going on the instrument, you have to be able to control your

| **17** |

There will be displays of the | *and* | **18** | of aboriginal peoples at today's event.

You will hear five writers giving advice to young people who want to start writing stories. For Questions **19–23**, choose from the list **A–F** what each speaker says. Use the letters only once. There is one extra letter which you do not need to use.

A   Concentrate on your writing.

B   Use simple language.

C   Write about your own life.

D   Write something original.

E   Keep a personal diary.

F   Do a lot of research.

Speaker 1	19
Speaker 2	20
Speaker 3	21
Speaker 4	22
Speaker 5	23

You will hear an interview with a young TV soap opera star, Jack Benton. For Questions **24–30**, choose the best answer **A**, **B** or **C**.

24   Jack got a role in the soap opera because
   A   he had a certificate in drama studies.
   B   one of his friends was a TV star.
   C   a TV star had just resigned.   24

25   Jack finds the most difficult part of his job is
   A   remembering his lines.
   B   pretending to be a bad person.
   C   working with famous people.   25

26   How does Jack avoid the bad effects of fame?
   A   He reads about other actors' experiences.
   B   He listens to his old friends.
   C   He follows his mother's advice.   26

27   What does Jack say about the clothes he wears?
   A   They are light-coloured.
   B   They are expensive.
   C   They are fashionable.   27

28   What does Jack value most in his friends.
   A   They help him to relax.
   B   They listen to his problems.
   C   They protect him from his fans.   28

29   What is Jack's reason for not going to the gym?
   A   He prefers team sports.
   B   He is too busy.
   C   He thinks it is unnecessary.   29

30   Jack's dream for the future is
   A   to become a cinema actor.
   B   to win a TV prize.
   C   to become world-famous.   30

PAPER 5   Speaking (14 minutes)

(3 minutes)

Answer these questions:

What do you enjoy doing in your free time?
Has your choice of freetime activities changed over the years?
Where do you like to go on holiday?
Is there a part of the world you would particularly like to visit? Why?

PART 2 (3 or 4 minutes)

Responsible jobs (compare, contrast and speculate)

Turn to pictures 1 and 2 on page 160 which show people doing responsible jobs.

Candidate A, compare and contrast these photographs, and say what type of person you need to be to do those jobs. You have a minute to do this.

Candidate B, could you do either of these jobs?

Making things (compare and contrast)

Turn to pictures 1 and 2 on page 161 which show people on holiday.

Candidate B, compare and contrast these photographs, and say how difficult these things are to make. You have a minute to do this.

Candidate A, are you good at making things?

PART 3 (3 or 4 minutes)

Discussion group (discuss and evaluate)

Turn to the pictures on page 162 which show ideas for a discussion group at your college. Students will have the opportunity to participate in a discussion with guest speakers who will be invited once a month. Look at the suggested discussion topics for the first three months.

What kind of advice may students need in each area? Which three areas do you think are the most urgent? How popular will these subjects be with students? What type of questions might students ask the speakers?

PART 4 (3 or 4 minutes)

Answer these questions:

What discussion subject interests you the most?
How difficult can it be to discuss these subjects with adults?
Why is it important to discuss these subjects?
What well-known personality would you invite to a discussion group?
How could you organise a discussion group?

TEST 5

PAPER 1 Reading (1 hour 15 minutes)

PART 1 You are going to read an article about a man who went on a training course for rangers in a wildlife reserve in Africa. Choose from the list **A–I** the sentence which best summarises each part (**1–7**) of the article. There is one extra sentence which you do not need to use. There is an example at the beginning (**0**).

Mark your answers **on the separate answer sheet**.

A	This is the situation the professionals fear.	**E**	This was an opportunity to see the wider picture.
B	This is a realistic assessment of the situation.	**F**	This was an unexpected achievement.
C	This was a good opportunity to sample certain conditions.	**G**	This is why it's important to keep your distance.
D	This was a chance to share the experiences of others.	**H**	This was a mistake not to be repeated.
		I	This was an essential skill to master.

RANGER TRAINING

Mark Thompson went to one of Africa's top wildlife reserves to take part in a training course for park rangers.

0 _____ I _____

As the buffalo charged towards me, I raised the rifle to my shoulder, tried to steady my arm, took aim and fired. The bullet hit it square in the chest, saving us from the dangerous attack, or least it would have done if this had been for real. The hole in the paper target was proof of that. I was in Africa to learn some of the skills that a park ranger requires and, although I have no love of guns, knowing how and when to shoot is a must.

1 _____

We were practising using real guns and bullets in the safety of a dried-up river bed, under the instruction of a real park ranger called Rick. 'Animals have a flight zone and a fight zone,' he explained. 'Get up close to them and they will run away, but at a certain point, if you get too close, they will turn and fight.'

2 _____

Apparently the danger when travelling is that you might suddenly come across an animal unexpectedly and surprise it, and buffaloes are the ones that scare the rangers most. 'Elephants usually stop short when they charge, but the buffalo just keeps on going, you have to shoot,' Rick warned us.

3 _____

Rick gave out such pieces of useful, common-sense advice at regular intervals. 'Don't stray too far from the camp,' he warned us. I looked around at the four large tents and ring of stones that marked the campfire under a great marula tree. Whilst all the holidaymakers in the safari lodge enjoyed hotel-style comforts, we had oil lamps and showered under a

bucket which was suspended from a tree. But I wasn't tempted to swap the simplicity of the camp for a hotel room, because in the camp I really felt a part of the bush.

4 _____

'One night a pride of lions came into the camp after we had gone to bed,' Michael from Chicago told me. He was one of a party from the USA who were making a return visit to the camp. The four of us on the ranger training course listened avidly to their tales from the wild side. 'The cubs were playing with the tent ropes.' As he continued, I made a mental note to sleep with my gun next to me.

5 _____

Soon I was in the mood for some adventures of my own. The days ahead were divided between lessons in ranger skills, and excursions into the bush. These tours, made either on foot or by four-wheel drive vehicle, began at the crack of dawn. They provided an opportunity not only to take in the wide variety of wildlife on the reserve, but also to gain an understanding of the whole ecosystem and the role of the ranger in that.

6 _____

Although I doubt if I'll ever be ready for a lone stroll across lion country, the course has at least increased my chances of survival. One afternoon, Rick let me take the wheel of the jeep and use my usually dreadful sense of direction to find our way back to camp. To my great astonishment I managed it, and realised that I was starting to make some sense of the landscape that had at first all looked the same.

7 _____

I had also learned that only a handful of dedicated and skilled individuals can really make it as a true professional in this business. What was called a ranger training course was really a lesson in ranger appreciation. There was no way that any of us would ever come close to being ready to take on any of their duties for real.

PART 2   You are going to read a article about a group of engineering students. For Questions **8–14**, choose the correct answer **A, B, C** or **D**.

Mark your answers **on the separate answer sheet**.

Fast-track Studies

Students at Birmingham University have found the drive to succeed – by building their own racing car.

Formula one motor racing is very much an international sport. Many of the leading formula one racing teams choose to base their operations in Britain, however. This is surprising because Britain no longer has a car manufacturing industry of any great significance. So why do the formula one teams choose to work there? In part the answer lies in the long tradition of mechanical engineering in British universities which continue to turn out highly-skilled graduates in the subject.

At Birmingham University, for example, the engineering department has specialised in preparing students for a career in the motor-racing industry. Students at the University have designed and built a single-seater racing car as part of their course. Each third-year student took sole responsibility for a section of the car, for example, the engine, bodywork or brakes, and the work was assessed as part of the students' final degree mark. Even more exciting for the students is the fact that the team building the car also gets to race it against teams from other universities.

This October, Martin Corsham, the student responsible for the engine on last year's course, is starting work as a trainee with one of the world's leading formula one teams. It is a dream job that makes every other mechanical engineering student in the country feel more than slightly envious. More significantly, it's a job that 21-year-old Corsham is
30 **adamant** he would not have got without the hands-on experience he gained at Birmingham.

'I've worked on cars since I was a kid,' he says, 'but this was the first engine that I'd worked on completely on my own. I took what was basically a motorcycle engine and turned it into an engine for the racing car.'

Corsham is clearly a true obsessive. He worked on the engine for at least three hours a day throughout his final year at university. The project finally came to a head the day before the car's official test run on April 22nd. Until that day, the engine had never actually run in the car itself. They eventually got it going at dawn after a desperate all-night session. 'But what a night!' Corsham says. 'I don't think I've got words to describe what it felt like, that feeling of great pride when it actually started. The most satisfying thing though was actually getting to drive the car. I was the first person who got the chance to drive the car with my engine in it, it was wonderful.'

Ian Stewart, who was responsible for the bodywork on the car, also found the whole experience very valuable, if a little frustrating. 'It's difficult relying on other people finalising their part before you can do yours,' he remembers. Stewart spent his whole Christmas holidays producing a model of the bodywork at home. He returned to college to find a few crucial details on other parts of the car had been changed and he had to start again.

The idea for the racing car programme originally came from the students themselves. Reading about an annual competition for racing-car builders in Detroit, USA, students on the course decided that they too would be capable of designing and building their own car. The university was quick to see the value of the idea and gave its backing.

Last May, the team took the car they had built to Detroit. Although the team was new to the competition, and had received relatively little funding compared to their rivals, their car impressed the judges. The university now plans to make the
71 project a regular feature of the course. **It** has proved very successful, not only as a practical demonstration of the students' theoretical studies, but also in allowing them to get their hands dirty and impress future employers.

8   On the Birmingham University course, each of the students

   A   builds a complete racing car.
   B   works with professional racing drivers.
   C   is expected to be successful in races.
   D   has a separate area of responsibility.

9   How do other students view Martin's new job?

   A   They are jealous of him.
   B   They are encouraged by it.
   C   They are proud of him.
   D   They are surprised by it.

10   'adamant' in line 30 describes a feeling of

   A   certainty.
   B   gratitude.
   C   satisfaction.
   D   modesty.

11   Which part of the project did Martin find most rewarding?

   A   working without assistance
   B   the last-minute preparations
   C   the moment the engine started
   D   driving the finished car

12   What did Ian Stewart find most difficult about the project?

   A   working in the holidays
   B   being dependent on other people
   C   producing a model of the car
   D   getting the details right

13   Where did the idea of the racing-car project come from?

   A   racing-car builders in Detroit
   B   staff at the university
   C   students on the course
   D   local employers

14   What does 'it' refer to in line 71?

   A   the car
   B   the course
   C   the project
   D   the university

You are going to read an extract from a book about a biking adventure. Seven paragraphs have been removed from the extract. Choose the most suitable paragraph from the list **A–H** for each gap (**15–20**). There is one extra paragraph which you do not need to use. There is an example at the beginning (**0**).

Mark your answers **on the separate answer sheet**.

Bikes on Kilimanjaro

We had succeeded in reaching the top of the mountain with our bikes still in working order. The next challenge was going to be coming down. We melted enough snow to provide us with water for the descent.

0	H

Then the whole lot was dropped into the top of my rucksack. The tent was plastered with ice, which added to the weight.

15	

And we had the bikes on top of that. When we pulled our bikes out of the snow to make our conclusive exit from the mountain, the sun was dropping down with increasing speed towards the black cliffs of Uhuru Peak and there was total silence.

16	

Nevertheless, our immediate objective had been fulfilled: that of cycling to Uhuru Peak. Unfortunately, much excitement and experimentation with the bicycles had to be abandoned.

17	

But principally, we had not done everything we had planned with our bikes because of the constraints of time in the modern society 3,000 miles away to which we were bound. Before starting the descent, we sat down to consider what we had gained from this experience.

18	

And only by living under stress with others can we form true bonds. It was certainly sad to leave Kibo summit, but we were in no doubt that there would be other adventures. Setting off down a mountain towards warmth and safety normally encourages a spring in the step.

19	

The combined weight of rider, bike and rucksack was over 130 kilograms; a lot for a pair of brakes to hold in normal conditions. I was sitting as far back as possible on the bike seat, keeping the weight as far rearwards as possible on the steep slope. I could just reach the handlebars with outstretched fingers.

20	

After that incident we experimented with other varying modes of downhill travel. Most ended with wild, uncontrollable slides and somersaults. But with every metre descended we felt better. Until we suddenly realised that our adventures on the mountain side were being observed from below. A crowd of mountain climbers had been following our every fall through binoculars!

A   Part of the reason for this had been our physical state. We had suffered a number of minor injuries on the way up, which had delayed our ascent. Getting to the top had left us with little energy for any extra bicycle riding.

B   However, that afternoon I was barely capable of lifting one foot above the other. In the first section of our descent there were many large rocks, so we were carrying our bikes down. At this point, I decided to try to ride the bike down, something that ended in disaster.

C   It was so quiet and calm that I could almost hear the creak of ice in the northern glacier. It was sad to say goodbye to the peak because we were leaving the adventure before we had really got started on the more exciting bits.

D   What I didn't realise until the whole ensemble was travelling at high speed, was that I couldn't see where I was going. The rucksack I was wearing on my chest had been pushed upwards into my face, leaving me totally sightless.

E   Instead of that, the bike turned over and the large rucksack took off down the slope in a series of giant hops. Picking up the bike, I wondered whether I'd ever recover the sack.

F   When we'd got everything packed up, we found we had the biggest and heaviest loads we'd ever seen. Each of us had one of the huge expedition rucksacks to carry, stuffed to the brim.

G   In spite of the sadness we felt, we knew that we had learnt a little more about ourselves and a drop more about other people. It is only by pushing ourselves to our limits that we get to explore ourselves.

H   This added up to several pints of valuable liquid in plastic containers, which weighed a ton. Sleeping bags, assorted socks and spare layers of clothing were packed away.

You are going to read a magazine article about successful young people. For Questions **21–35**, choose from the people (**A–D**). The people may be chosen more than once. There is an example at the beginning (**0**).

Mark your answers **on the separate answer sheet**.

A	Justin Weston
B	Tom Hall
C	Adam Huntley
D	Josh Rendell

Who

has been successful at writing?	**0**	*B*
thinks criticism has a positive effect on him?	**21**	
found a job was easier than expected?	**22**	
has seen his income increase?	**23**	
is grateful to a teacher?	**24**	
was influenced by the area where he lived?	**25**	
wants to change the responsibilities of a job?	**26**	
considers experience more important than qualifications?	**27**	
always had a clear sense of purpose?	**28**	
does not want to be a role model?	**29**	
is worried about leaving others in charge?	**30**	
did not accept a job he was offered?	**31**	
thinks his success may have a positive effect on others?	**32**	
is unhappy about the calls he receives?	**33**	
is not liked by some fellow workers?	**34**	
is in contact with young people in his area?	**35**	

Justin Weston is one of the most hotly discussed young British artists. After a childhood in the south of England, he discovered his passion for art while at secondary school in Scotland, where the whole family had moved when he was fifteen. 'I owe my success to the arts instructor who pushed me all the way to Arts College,' he says. The move from England to Scotland also brought him into direct contact with the landscape that was to become his main subject matter. Mr Weston looks set to become one of his generation's great painters, but his style is not universally popular, as a number of negative comments from colleagues has shown. 'Such comments only give me more courage to do new and exciting things and to paint more effectively,' he says.

Tom Hall is a political correspondent. He has built up a glittering career in television journalism since graduating from London University in 1993. Even at university, he knew where he was going. While fellow history students enjoyed an active social life, Tom performed in plays and edited the student newspaper. When he graduated, he turned down job offers from the national papers for the exciting performance aspects of television reporting. He found the work much less demanding than he had thought it would be. 'I was able to turn my attention to writing as well,' he says. Days after publication, his thriller, *Shadows*, has won critical acclaim. The only thing Tom Hall dislikes about his job is finding an average of thirty messages on his answering machine every day. 'Mostly from newspaper editors asking my opinion,' he says.

MEET THE RISING TALENTS

WITH CAREERS VARYING FROM FARMING TO POLITICS, THESE YOUNG ACHIEVERS – MOST STILL IN THEIR TWENTIES – ARE OUR TIPS FOR THE MOVERS OF TOMORROW …

Adam Huntley is a gardener. It is refreshing to meet a successful young person who is not happy at the thought of being seen as a leader of a generation. 'I don't like that at all,' he says. But the facts speak for themselves. At the age of 26, Adam has just become Head Gardener at Cromart, one of the most renowned gardens in England. 'My approach as Head Gardener will be different from what has gone on so far,' he says, 'the modern Head Gardener also has to be involved in attracting visitors.' Adam has been awarded a grant for a trip to the Caribbean, where he hopes to find a number of plants to enrich the Cromart garden. 'I am pleased at the prospect of travelling,' he says, 'but I'm also nervous about letting somebody else take over my job.'

Josh Rendell is a farmer. Owner and manager of a large dairy and arable crop farm, 29-year-old Josh finds he is the youngest of all farmers in the area. In 1991, he and his three brothers inherited the land from their father. Since then, he has reduced costs and increased efficiency to such an extent that his profits have doubled. Josh has a geography degree from Exeter University and a degree in business management, but most of what he has learnt, he says, came from his day-to-day work on the job. His recreations include organising visits to the farm for children in local schools, but his central role is running the farm well. 'If your business is healthy,' he says, 'it can benefit the local community.'

You **must** answer this question.

1 You are planning a camping holiday with a friend who has sent you a letter with a Camping Site advertisement. Read the letter and the advertisement together with the notes. Then write to Willows Camping Site asking for the information which your friend suggests and adding any relevant questions of your own.

> *This would be a good place for our holiday but we need to find out more! I'm busy helping in my parent's shop. Could you write for more details using my notes? May be we won't need to take our tents. Can you think of anything else we need to ask?*
>
> *See you soon.*

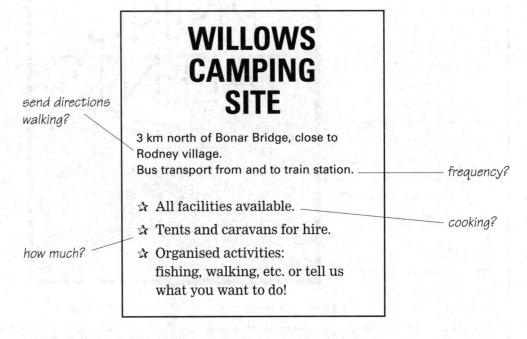

send directions walking?

WILLOWS CAMPING SITE

3 km north of Bonar Bridge, close to Rodney village.
Bus transport from and to train station. — *frequency?*

☆ All facilities available. — *cooking?*

☆ Tents and caravans for hire.

how much? ☆ Organised activities:
fishing, walking, etc. or tell us what you want to do!

Write a **letter** of between **120** and **180** words in an appropriate. Do not write any addresses.

Write an answer to **one** of the Questions **2–5** in this part. Write your answer in **120–180** words in an appropriate style.

2   You see this announcement in an international magazine for young people learning English.

> **Take my advice ...**
> Write an article telling other students the things that have worked for you in learning English.
> You should describe any method, books or people who have helped you and explain how these could help other students.

Write your **article**.

3   You have decided to enter a short story competition. The competition rules say that the story must **begin** with these words:

It all began when the phone rang.

Write your **story**.

4   This is part of a letter you have received from a friend in another country.

> *We're doing a project at school about how computers are changing people's lives in different countries. Please could you write me a short report about your country, saying how computers are changing things and how people feel about it? I can then include this in my project.*

Write your **report**.

5   Answer **one** of the following two questions based on your reading of **one** of the set books.

Either (a) Which character in the book or one of the short stories you have read did you like least? Write a **composition**, explaining which character you have chosen and why.

Or (b) A magazine for young people has a page where readers can give their opinions about books they have read. Write a short **article** for the magazine, saying what type of young people would enjoy the book and why.

Use of English (1 hour 15 minutes)

For Questions **1–15**, read the text below and decide which answer **A**, **B**, **C** or **D** best fits each space. There is an example at the beginning (**0**).

Mark your answers **on the separate answer sheet**.

Example:

| **0** | **A** origin | **B** age | **C** spring | **D** growth |

| **0** | **A** | **B** | **C** | **D** |

MUSIC

Nobody knows for certain what the (**0**) ..... of music was. Music is certainly older than poetry and painting but as early man had no way of (**1**) ..... it, we can only (**2**) ..... what it sounded like. Watching a child (**3**) ..... on a drum with its hands or a (**4**) ..... of wood, it is easy to see that this is the simplest of instruments. It does not (**5**) ..... much effort to produce a rhythm on it.

Wall paintings show what some of the first instruments (**6**) ..... like. Early civilisations had already discovered the three basic (**7**) ..... of producing music: blowing into a tube, striking an object, and scraping a string. We know that western music comes from the (**8**) ..... Greeks. The musical scales we use now are (**9**) ..... on certain sequences of notes which the Greeks used to create a particular (**10**) ....

Until the sixteenth century, most players of instruments were (**11**) ..... performers, but as music became more (**12**) ....., orchestras and musical groups began to (**13**) .... This (**14**) ..... about the writing of music to be played by several musicians at one time. This can certainly be (**15**) ..... the birth of modern music.

1	**A** recording	**B** playing	**C** producing	**D** performing
2	**A** think	**B** reckon	**C** guess	**D** realise
3	**A** hitting	**B** knocking	**C** crashing	**D** banging
4	**A** slice	**B** point	**C** piece	**D** shape
5	**A** make	**B** call	**C** take	**D** do
6	**A** looked	**B** appeared	**C** felt	**D** sounded
7	**A** forms	**B** manners	**C** systems	**D** ways
8	**A** ancient	**B** old	**C** aged	**D** antique
9	**A** raised	**B** based	**C** established	**D** supported
10	**A** spirit	**B** temper	**C** mood	**D** humour
11	**A** separate	**B** lonely	**C** unique	**D** single
12	**A** widespread	**B** enlarged	**C** expanded	**D** extended
13	**A** turn	**B** appear	**C** spring	**D** be
14	**A** produced	**B** affected	**C** caused	**D** brought
15	**A** appointed	**B** called	**C** decided	**D** named

For Questions **16–30**, read the text below and think of the word which best fits each space. Use only **one** word in each space. There is an example at the beginning (**0**).

Write your answers **on the separate answer sheet**.

Example:	**0**	*one*

RUNNING

Running is (**0**) .... of the cheapest and most effective forms of exercise. When you first (**16**) .... up the sport, it is important to build up your strength slowly. You should, however, plan to go out for (**17**) .... least thirty minutes, running for a minute and walking for a minute. (**18**) .... this seems like a long time, you should try running (**19**) .... a partner as this will help you to (**20**) .... going.

It is a good idea to run on grass rather (**21**) .... hard surfaces. This will help you to avoid injury to your muscles which may not be (**22**) .... to this kind of exercise. You (**23**) .... to wear clothes that are both waterproof and lightweight and you should take care over your choice of footwear. This is (**24**) .... the right kind of shoes are absolutely essential for running.

Make (**25**) .... you buy them from a shop (**26**) .... the staff are trained to help you to match the shoe to things (**27**) .... the weight and shape of your foot. Don't be influenced (**28**) .... brand names, but look for comfort. You should allow a centimetre (**29**) .... the tip of your big toe and the end of the shoe. The average shoe is good for 200–300 miles, so you should be prepared to buy a new (**30**) .... regularly.

For Questions **31–40**, complete the second sentence so that it has a similar meaning to the first sentence, using the word given. **Do not change the word given.** You must use between two and five words, including the word given. Here is an example (**0**).

Example: **0** You should book their ticket today to be sure of getting a seat.

> **had**
>
> To be sure of getting a seat, ... your ticket today.

The gap can be filled by the words 'you had better book' so you write:

0	*you had better book*

Write **only the missing words** on the separate answer sheet.

---

31 If Amy had arrived a moment later, she would have missed the start of the film.

time

Amy arrived just .... the start of the film.

32 Guests are asked to say if they prefer tea or coffee with their breakfast.

rather

Guests are asked to say if .... tea or coffee with their breakfast.

33 Mrs Parker expressed her thanks for all the help she'd received.

grateful

Mrs Parker said that .... all the help she'd received.

34 People say that there are bears living in these mountains.

said

Bears .... in these mountains.

35 Not many people read magazines about stamp collecting these days.

widely

Magazines about stamp collecting .... these days.

36 John will only answer if you ring the doorbell twice.

unless

John .... you ring the doorbell twice.

37 Too tired to continue, Phil stopped walking.

carry

Phil couldn't .... he was too tired.

38 Trevor decided to wait and only book his flight at the last minute.

put

Trevor decided .... his flight until the last minute.

39 You must not waste any time in applying for a visa.

soon

You must apply for a visa .... possibly can.

40 We'll only eat indoors if it rains.

long

As .... rain, we'll eat outdoors.

For Questions **41–55**, read the text below and look carefully at each line. Some of the lines are correct, and some have a word which should not be there.

If a line is correct, put a tick (✔) by the number **on the separate answer sheet**. If a line has a word which should not be there, write the word **on the separate answer sheet**. There are examples at the beginning (**0** and **00**).

Examples:	0	to
	00	✔

STUDENT'S WEEK

0	....	In my town, students like to celebrating Students' Week,
00	....	which begins with a party on the first day of spring.
41	....	There is a whole week of activities which organised by all
42	....	the schools in the area, and students like to invite them
43	....	their parents and teachers to the party so that everyone
44	....	can have a really good time and enjoy of the celebrations.
45	....	First, I am going to tell you something about the preparations
46	....	made up in advance. Students build stands, which are
47	....	large tables where they can be put all the food
48	....	for the party. Music is very important, so that the students
49	....	who can play instruments get together with to practise the
50	....	songs they are going to play. Everyone looks forward to
51	....	Students' Week because it is such a fun for the young and
52	....	also for the old. Even so, when it rains, the celebrations are
53	....	not spoilt as it is always possible to move into the tents
54	....	which students put up just in the case they are needed.
55	....	If you think ever visit my town in spring, come and join us.

For Questions **56–65**, read the text below. Use the word given in capitals at the end of each line to form a word that fits in the space in the same line. There is an example at the beginning (**0**). Write your answers **on the separate answer sheet.**

Example:	0	*visitors*

RULES FOR WILDLIFE WATCHERS

There are a few rules that all (**0**) ...*visitors*.... to the wildlife reserves   **VISIT**

should observe. (**56**) .... these rules is necessary   **FOLLOW**

if people want to enjoy themselves and have an (**57**) ....   **FORGET**

experience. First of all, it is (**58**) .... to leave your car   **ADVISE**

in the car park so as to cause as little (**59**) .... as possible   **DISTURB**

to the varied wildlife. The animals can be easily (**60**) ....   **FRIGHT**

by unexpected noises, (**61**) .... those made by   **PARTICULAR**

machines. Secondly, people need to be (**62**) .... if they   **PATIENCE**

want to see the animals in their natural (**63**) ....   **SURROUND**

This often means that people have to put up with (**64**) ....   **PLEASANT**

weather conditions and (**65**) .... insects.   **ANNOY**

Listening (40 minutes)

You will hear people talking in eight different situations. For Questions **1–8**, choose the best answer **A**, **B** or **C**.

1   You hear a man talking about a new public building.
    What does the building contain?
    A   a museum
    B   a library
    C   a leisure centre

    `1`

2   You overhear a man talking.
    What is the man doing?
    A   giving advice
    B   telling a story
    C   asking someone to do something

    `2`

3   You hear a man talking about a mountain.
    Why did he advise his friend not to climb it?
    A   The walk would be too long.
    B   His friend was not fit enough.
    C   The mountain paths were rough.

    `3`

4   You hear a man talking about a meal he had.
    What was unexpected about the meal?
    A   the amount of food
    B   the quality of the cooking
    C   the price he had to pay

    `4`

5   You hear a woman who works for a dance company.
    What is her role in the company?
    A   She trains the dancers.
    B   She selects new dancers.
    C   She organises the tours.

    `5`

6   You hear a manager talking about her employees.
    What does she expect them to do?
    A   check their own work
    B   work a fixed number of hours
    C   keep their skills up to date

    `6`

7   You hear an advertisement for a boat trip.
    What will customers get if they don't get to see dolphins?
    A   another trip on a boat
    B   their money back
    C   a free meal

    `7`

8   You hear a man talking about his job.
    What does he do now?
    A   He is a writer.
    B   He is an actor.
    C   He is a teacher.

    `8`

You will hear part of a radio programme about restaurants. For Questions **9–18**, complete the notes.

The Blue Restaurant

Best place to sit: ☐ **9**

What you can see: *The River Thames*

☐ **10**

Best thing to eat: ☐ **11**

Apple pie

Tamsin's Restaurant

Best place to sit: ☐ **12**

What you can see: *Shopping street*

☐ **13**

Best thing to eat: ☐ **14**

Mushroom soup

The River Restaurant

Best place to sit: ☐ **15**

What you can see: *The park*

☐ **16**

Best thing to eat: ☐ **17**

☐ **18**

You will hear five tour guides saying why tourists value their work. For Questions **19–23**, choose from the list **A–F** what each speaker says. Use the letters only once. There is one extra letter which you do not need to use.

Why tourists value my work

A   I speak several foreign languages.

B   I am a specialist on local museums.

C   I organise the tour myself.

D   I adapt my services to different age groups.

E   I offer tourists advice on entertainment.

F   I know the history of this area well.

Speaker 1	19
Speaker 2	20
Speaker 3	21
Speaker 4	22
Speaker 5	23

PART 4

You will hear a radio interview with Ella Webster, a fashion photographer. For Questions **24–30**, decide which of the statements are TRUE and which are FALSE and write T for **True** or F for **False** in the boxes provided.

24   Ella thinks travelling is an unpleasant part of her job.   `24`

25   Ella's problems are often caused by insensitive editors.   `25`

26   In Mauritius, Ella had no time to take all the planned photos.   `26`

27   A problem at the airport prevented the plane from landing at Nairobi.   `27`

28   After the landing in Uganda some of the luggage was lost.   `28`

29   The experience at Nairobi made Ella change some of her opinions.   `29`

30   At present, Ella is thinking about whether to change jobs.   `30`

PAPER 5

Speaking (14 minutes)

Answer these questions:

Tell us something about your reasons for studying English.
Tell us where and how you've learnt English.
Do you know any other foreign languages?
Which other language do you think will be most useful for you to learn?

PART 2 (3 or 4 minutes)

Taxis (compare, contrast and speculate)

Turn to pictures 1 and 2 on page 163 which show people who have chosen to travel by taxi.

Candidate A, compare and contrast these photographs, and say why you think the people have chosen to travel by taxi. You have a minute to do this.

Candidate B, do you often travel by taxi?

People and animals (compare, contrast and speculate)

Turn to pictures 1 and 2 on page 164 which show people and animals.

Candidate B, compare and contrast these photographs, and say how you think the people are feeling about the animals. You have a minute to do this.

Candidate A, do you like animals?

PART 3 (3 or 4 minutes)

Weekend activities (discuss and evaluate)

Turn to the pictures on page 165 which show ideas for special weekend activities at a college. The activities are designed to encourage young people to play and work in teams.

What team skills might students learn in each activity? Which activity do you think would encourage team spirit best?

PART 4 (3 or 4 minutes)

Answer these questions:

How much do you like working in teams?
What happens when a team member is not really making an effort?
When is it better to work individually instead of in a team?
Who is better at playing in teams, teenagers or children?
How do people study in your country, in groups or individually?
What team sports are popular in your country?

TEST 6

PART 1

You are going to read an extract from an article about rowing. Choose the most suitable heading from the list **A–I** for each part (**1–7**) of the extract. There is one extra heading which you do not need to use. There is an example at the beginning (**0**).

Mark your answers **on the separate answer sheet**.

A	The challenge of middle-age	**F**	Childhood impressions
B	A record broken	**G**	Learning to accept danger
C	A priority: understanding oneself	**H**	Wanted: an almost impossible challenge
D	The earliest successes	**I**	A decision taken
E	Unexpected success stories		

---

0   *I*

Planning what to do for one's birthday becomes increasingly difficult as one gets older, but I know how I will celebrate on October 9th next year. I intend to row the 2,900 miles from Tenerife to Barbados.

1

Many people have tried to row across the Atlantic and quite a few have managed it. It is clear from accounts of survivors that it is an exhausting test of endurance. Soldiers, sailors, housewives, Olympic rowers: the triumphant emerge from surprisingly varied quarters.

2

What is apparent, however, is that the main struggle takes place not in the muscles but in the mind. So, before fussing over such preliminaries as finding a crewmate and sponsorship to the tune of £50,000, I realised that first I had to explore my own mind and try to answer the obvious question of why I wanted to do something that most people would find frightening and painful.

3

When we are young we can afford to dream; as we grow older the gap widens between what we would like to do and what we actually can do. We come to the realisation that we either have to act now or dream on. After the age of forty, people respond to that realisation

in varying ways, and rowing across the Atlantic is one of them.

4

I have sailed, climbed, explored the Amazon and run marathons, but what I am looking for now is an endeavour that scares me and may not be within my capabilities. Such as racing across the Atlantic in a rowing boat.

5

Two Norwegian sailors were the first to row the Atlantic in 1896. They took 60 days and their achievement was unequalled until 1966, when two soldiers, John Ridgway and Chay Blyth, made it in 91 days.

6

It wasn't until the first Atlantic Rowing Race, in 1997, that New Zealanders Rob Hamill and Phil Stubbs shot across to Barbados in an incredible 41 days. This was less than half the time Ridgway and Blyth had taken.

7

As a schoolboy I had read about Blyth and Ridgway and about the innumerable hardships and setbacks they suffered. It was horrifying, and I concluded they were mad. Looking back at the book now, I see they thought so too. When people asked them why they had undertaken such a dangerous journey, they replied that every person had secret ambitions.

You are going to read a passage written by a zoologist. For Questions **8–14**, choose the correct answer **A**, **B**, **C** or **D**.

Mark your answers **on the separate answer sheet**.

Most children at the tender age of six or so are full of the most impractical schemes for becoming policemen, firemen or train drivers when they grow up. But when I was that age, I could not be bothered with such mundane ambitions. I knew exactly what I wanted to do, I was going to have my own zoo. At the time, this did not seem to me, and still does not seem, a very unreasonable idea. My friends and relatives, who had long found me strange because I showed little interest in anything that did not have fur or feathers, accepted this as just another manifestation of my strangeness. They felt that, if they ignored my often-repeated remarks about owning my own zoo, I would eventually grow out of it.

11 As the years passed, however, to the **bewilderment** of those friends and relatives, my resolve to have my own zoo grew greater and greater, and eventually, after going on a number of expeditions to bring back animals for other zoos, I felt the time was ripe to acquire my own.

From my latest trip to West Africa, I had brought back a considerable collection of animals which were living, temporarily I assured her, in my sister's suburban garden in Bournemouth. But after a number of unsuccessful attempts to convince local councils in various areas to support my plans, I began to investigate the possibility of starting my zoo on the island of Jersey in the English Channel.

I was given an introduction to a man named Hugh Fraser who, I was told, was a broad-minded, kindly soul. He would show me around the island and point out suitable sites. So, I flew to Jersey and was met by Hugh Fraser who drove us to his family home, probably one of the most beautiful old houses on the island. There was a huge walled garden with lots of outbuildings all built in the beautiful local stone which was the colour of autumn leaves glowing in the sunshine. Turning to my wife, I said: 'What a marvellous place for a zoo.'

If my host had promptly fainted on the spot, I could not have blamed him. The thought of creating the average person's idea of a zoo, with all the grey cement and iron bars, in such a lovely spot was horrible. To my astonishment, however, Hugh Fraser did not faint, but merely cocked an enquiring eyebrow at me and asked whether I really meant what I said. Slightly embarrassed, I replied that I had meant it, but added hastily that I realised that it was impossible. Hugh said he did not think it was as impossible as all that.

He went on to explain that the house and grounds were too big for him to keep up as a private individual, and so he wanted to move to a smaller place in England. Would I care to consider renting the property for the purpose of establishing my zoo? I could not imagine more attractive surroundings for my purpose, and by the time lunch was over, the bargain had been sealed.

The alarm displayed by all who knew me when this was announced can be imagined. The only exception to the general chorus of disapproval was my sister. Although she thought it a mad scheme, at least it would rid her back garden of the assorted jungle creatures who were beginning to put a great strain on her relationship with her neighbours.

8 How did the writer's friends and family react to his childhood ambition?

    A   They took no notice of it.
    B   They encouraged him in it.
    C   They tried to talk him out of it.
    D   They tried to interest him in other things.

9 What does the word 'bewilderment' in line 11 tell us about the attitude of friends and relatives to the writer as he grew up?

    A   They were pleasantly surprised by him.
    B   They became increasingly angry with him.
    C   They were shown to be right about his ideas.
    D   They didn't really understand his ambitions.

10 Why didn't the writer start a zoo in England?

    A   He had too many animals.
    B   His sister was against it.
    C   Nobody wanted to help him.
    D   He couldn't get permission.

11 Why was the writer introduced to Hugh Fraser?

    A   Hugh knew a lot about zoos.
    B   Hugh owned a number of houses.
    C   Hugh knew the island very well.
    D   Hugh had offered land for rent.

12 What was Hugh's initial reaction to the writer's comment about the walled garden?

    A   He was horrified at the prospect.
    B   He was surprised by the suggestion.
    C   He was too embarrassed to reply.
    D   He was interested in the idea.

13 What did the writer particularly like about the place he chose for his zoo?

    A   its size
    B   its price
    C   its setting
    D   its facilities

14 How did the writer's sister feel about the establishment of the zoo in Jersey?

    A   alarmed
    B   relieved
    C   supportive
    D   disappointed

You are going to read a magazine article about a woman who makes mirrors decorated with seashells. Six sentences have been removed from the article. Choose from the sentences **A–I** the one which fits each gap (**15–21**). There is one extra sentence which you do not need to use. There is an example at the beginning (**0**).

Mark your answers **on the separate answer sheet**.

MAKING MIRRORS

Viv Thomas used her exotic shell collection to embark on a new career making the decorated mirrors which she now sells all over the world.

Viv Thomas, together with her husband Clive, returned to Britain after nearly 30 years of living abroad with wonderful memories. **0**   *I*

Determined to use them rather than just keep them in a box or throw them out, Viv made a shell mirror for her bathroom. This was very much admired by friends and neighbours who came to visit her. **15**

That was two years ago. Viv now runs her own small mirror-making business. She buys shells from all over the world through a wholesale company and has converted a spare bedroom in her house into an office-cum-studio. **16**

A local carpenter makes frames for her and a glazier then fits the glass inside. Viv does everything else herself; the design, the initial painting of the frame and then the final making up. **17**

Clive is a banker and was able to advise Viv on deciding how much money should be invested when she decided to set up the business. Around £3000 was spent on shells alone. **18** Viv's main problem was knowing how to market her work more widely.

Local shops could only sell a small number because once they had added their profit margin, the mirrors became rather expensive. However, Viv has now made contact with another company that makes and sells mirrors of a different type. **19** At such events, the right sort of people get to see the mirrors and can order them directly.

Venturing into other areas, Viv plans to approach restaurants and hotels directly as she thinks her mirrors might be attractive to them. She has also taken a website on the Internet. **20** It means Viv doesn't have the expense of travelling around with her range of mirrors in the back of the car.

Viv reckons it will take another year before her business starts to make money. **21** She would like to employ someone to help her with the administration and preparation of the frames, for example, which would allow her to devote more time to the artistic side.

A Together they can afford to take stands at specialist exhibitions and craft fairs.

B This represents about one week's work and each mirror brings in anything between £100 and £400 for the business.

C As Viv discovered, it's a good idea to find a company willing to sell goods on your behalf.

D Before long, she was being asked to make mirrors for other people.

E But it didn't end there, Viv also had to think about equipment such as the heavy-duty boxes needed to send the mirrors abroad.

F She works there, surrounded by shells of every shape and colour and the other materials needed to make the mirrors.

G Once this happens, she feels she will be able to concentrate on the side of the business she enjoys.

H This is a very economical way of selling.

I She also brought back a huge collection of sea shells collected from beaches around the Indian Ocean.

PART 4

You are going to read an article about student accommodation in which four college students talk about the place they live. For Questions **22–35**, choose from the people (**A–D**). The people may be chosen more than once. There is an example at the beginning (**0**).

Mark your answers **on the separate answer sheet**.

Which student says ...?

My accommodation seems quite expensive.	**0**	*A*
I have plenty of storage space.	**22**	
I have reason to regret a decision.	**23**	
My college doesn't provide accommodation.	**24**	
My room is maintained to a high standard.	**25**	
I have washing facilities in my room.	**26**	
I would like to have more independence.	**27**	
I had to buy some extra electrical equipment.	**28**	
I would like to have more private space.	**29**	
It's easy to keep in touch with people here.	**30**	
My room is not very well-furnished.	**31**	
I'm expected to do my share of the housework.	**32**	
This is the only place where I can afford to live.	**33**	
I save money by doing my own cooking.	**34**	
There are good recreational facilities nearby.	**35**	

A	Matthew Wren

I live in what's called a hall of residence where I get full board as well as a room. It's not exactly what you call cheap, though. I pay £87 per week for my single room and three meals a day. This also includes the use of a washing machine and ironing board. But I can't complain because my room has just been re-carpeted, the furniture's new and the cleaner comes in daily. The main drawback is sharing the bathroom with nine other students and we don't have any kitchen facilities. The first thing I did when I arrived was buy myself a mini-fridge, so I could have cool drinks whenever I wanted. But, we're on the university network, so I have access to the Internet and free e-mail from my room, and we get room phones so I can ring friends around the campus for nothing.

B	Kerry Dunnock

The city where I study is appalling for cheap accommodation, and the college has nothing of its own to offer you, but I was lucky. I found a room in a nice little terraced house with central heating which I share with three other girls. I have a yearly contract with a private landlady and I pay £220 a month for my study bedroom. This is not bad as it also has a large walk-in wardrobe where I put all my stuff. I share the bathroom, kitchen and a small living room with the other girls, and we split all the bills between us. We tried to make a rota for the washing up, cleaning and putting out the rubbish, but it's not always strictly followed. Cooking your own food is much cheaper than eating at college, and I like it because I have what I want when I want it.

C	Becky Martin

I live in a college-owned self-catering block. There's not much luxury, but I get value for money. For my £38 per week rent, I get a reasonably-sized room with an old wardrobe, a tiny desk, one shelf, a rather stained carpet and a sink. When I first moved in, I probably spent more on decoration than I did on food. My only real complaint, though, was that I had to buy a new pillow because the one I was provided with felt like a plastic bag full of old towels. I share the kitchen and bathroom with six other girls. One of them has a TV in her room, but she is a bit possessive about it. The fridge is not huge, so you're always trying to squeeze your food into the last remaining inch of space. I twice set off the fire alarm by burning my dinner, so tended to give up on cooking after that. We eat a lot of take-aways. In the next block, there's a games room where we hang out which has things like table football and satellite TV if you need a break from studying.

D	Karl Yorat

I made the big mistake of going to a college fairly near my home. It isn't so much the course that I don't like, but the fact that I'm stuck at my parents' house so I don't feel in touch with what's going on at campus. In some ways I'm lucky because I'm not paying out all the money for food and rent that other people have to find, and I have someone to do my washing, but I don't have the same amount of freedom or privacy as the people who're living away from home. I even have to share a room with my younger brother. When I told my parents I wanted to move out and go into college accommodation, they said they'd stop supporting me financially. So, in the end, I had to give up the idea, that hasn't made any of us very happy.

PART 1   You **must** answer this question.

1   You are planning to do a computer course with a friend who has sent you a letter with
    a school advertisement. Read the letter and the advertisement together with the notes.
    Then write to the school asking for the information which your friend suggests and
    adding any relevant questions of your own.

> *I think this may be just the kind of course we want. Could you write to the school for more details? I've made some notes and maybe you can think of other points.*
>
> *See you when I come back from holiday!*

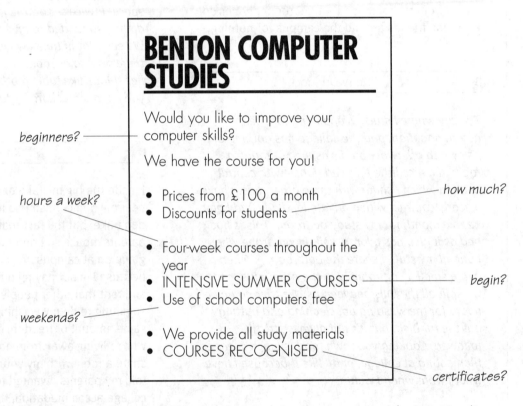

Write a **letter** of between **120** and **180** words in an appropriate style. Do not write
any addresses.

PART 2

Write an answer to **one** of the Questions **2–5** in this part. Write your answer in **120–180** words in an appropriate style.

2 An international magazine for English learners of your age is organising a writing competition. The rules of the competition say you must write a composition with this title about a musical or theatrical performance you have seen.

A live performance I will never forget

Write your **composition**.

3 A small town in your country is hoping to attract foreign tourists. You have been asked to write an article for an international travel magazine describing the town briefly and explaining what tourists can see and do there.

Write your **article**.

4 You see this advertisement in an international newspaper. You are interested in applying for the job.

An English language newspaper needs reporters in all countries to write about local events in the areas of sport, fashion or the arts. If you are interested, please write to us explaining why you would be a good person to do this job and what you could write about.

Write your **letter of application**. Do not include any addresses.

5 Answer **one** of the following two questions based on your reading of **one** of the set books.

Either (a) A television company is planning to turn the book you have read into a television serial aimed at teenagers. You have been asked to write a report saying whether you think this is a good idea and what changes might be necessary to the plot, the setting or the characters.

Write your **report**.

Or (b) An Internet magazine has a page where people can recommend books they have read to others. Write an article for the magazine saying what you liked and disliked about the book you have read and what type of people you think might enjoy it.

Write your **article**.

Use of English (1 hour 15 minutes)

For Questions **1–15**, read the text below and decide which answer **A**, **B**, **C** or **D** best fits each space. There is an example at the beginning (**0**).

Mark your answers **on the separate answer sheet**.

Example:

| 0 | **A** further | **B** older | **C** greater | **D** more |

TEDDY BEARS

The history of the teddy bear goes back no (**0**) ..... than 1903. In that year, a cartoon (**1**) ..... in an American newspaper showing President Theodore (Teddy) Roosevelt (**2**) ..... to shoot a bear cub on a hunting expedition. Soon after this, an enterprising toy shop owner in New York made some toy bears and (**3**) ..... them in his shop window with a sign that (**4**) ..... 'Teddy's bear'. These bears proved to be so popular that they soon sold (**5**) ....., and it wasn't long before a factory was established to (**6**) ..... advantage of the great (**7**) ..... for these new toys.

At about the same time, the Steiff toy factory in Germany had introduced a (**8**) ..... of soft toys, made (**9**) ..... mohair and wood shavings, with movable heads and limbs. (**10**) ..... the popularity of teddy bears in the USA, Steiff decided to (**11**) ..... making these as well and they were modelled (**12**) ..... the real bears in Stuttgart zoo. It is these early Steiff bears that are now most eagerly sought (**13**) ..... by collectors.

These days, teddy bears are a good investment for people who want to sell them years later at a much (**14**) ..... price. However, it's obvious that most teddy bear lovers collect them for (**15**) ..... rather than profit.

1	**A** remarked	**B** approached	**C** appeared	**D** reported
2	**A** defending	**B** reversing	**C** denying	**D** refusing
3	**A** displayed	**B** published	**C** introduced	**D** demonstrated
4	**A** said	**B** wrote	**C** spoke	**D** named
5	**A** out	**B** up	**C** off	**D** away
6	**A** take	**B** find	**C** make	**D** get
7	**A** claim	**B** order	**C** demand	**D** request
8	**A** grade	**B** chain	**C** kind	**D** range
9	**A** along with	**B** down from	**C** up for	**D** out of
10	**A** Given	**B** As	**C** Although	**D** Since
11	**A** enter	**B** put	**C** set	**D** begin
12	**A** on	**B** at	**C** with	**D** in
13	**A** through	**B** to	**C** after	**D** for
14	**A** hotter	**B** harder	**C** heavier	**D** higher
15	**A** charm	**B** purpose	**C** choice	**D** pleasure

For Questions **16–30**, read the text below and think of the word which best fits each space. Use only **one** word in each space. There is an example at the beginning (**0**).

Write your answers **on the separate answer sheet**.

Example:	**0**	*have*

HOLIDAY READING

Tourists in the British holiday resort of Blackpool (**0**) .... no excuse to be without a book to read on the beach this summer, (**16**) .... to the launch of the UK's first mobile seafront library. For the two months of high season, two local students will be pushing a multicoloured barrow (**17**) .... the deckchairs and sunshades on the beach, handing (**18**) .... novels and reading advice to some of the resort's sixteen million visitors.

The scheme, (**19**) .... has been launched by the local council's library and information service, relies (**20**) .... second-hand books, specially donated (**21**) .... the people of the town. This means that borrowers can either keep, return (**22**) .... swap the books. In (**23**) .... event of poor weather the two students, Catherine and Melanie, will be offering indoor storytelling sessions for children instead.

Both women have been selected for (**24**) .... combination of good humour, love of books and fitness. They will be trying to persuade people sitting on the beach to (**25**) .... down their newspapers and (**26**) .... into a book instead. Holiday reading, they insist, isn't just to (**27**) .... with relaxation, it's a chance to read things you (**28**) .... not otherwise have time to try. The only problem that Catherine and Melanie foresee is that they might (**29**) .... out of books. (**30**) .... the idea is a success, other resorts could soon be following Blackpool's example.

For Questions **31–40**, complete the second sentence so that it has a similar meaning to the first sentence, using the word given. **Do not change the word given.** You must use between two and five words, including the word given. Here is an example (**0**).

Example: 0   It was difficult for Angela to understand why Peter had gone away.

   found

   Angela .... why Peter had gone away.

The gap can be filled by the words 'found it difficult to understand' so you write:

| 0 | *found it difficult to understand* |

Write **only the missing words** on the separate answer sheet.

---

31   The police were there to make sure that the crowd did not invade the football pitch.

   prevent

   The police were there to .... the football pitch.

32   During the storm, they did not let the children leave the school building.

   allowed

   During the storm, the children .... the school building

33   The heavy summer rainfall has caused severe floods.

   brought

   Severe floods .... the heavy summer rainfalls.

34   It is not advisable for Jane to request a bank loan at the moment.

   ought

   Jane .... a bank loan at the moment.

35   Paul did not visit the Smiths because he didn't know where they lived.

   if

   Paul would have visited the Smiths .... where they lived.

36   Mary made mistakes because she refused to listen to advice.

   resulted

   Mary's mistakes .... refusal to listen to advice.

37   They say the government is considering the introduction of a new tax on fuel.

   said

   The government .... the introduction of a new tax on fuel.

38   George's health is better than I had been led to believe.

   as

   George's health .... I had been led to believe.

39   Although Tom eats large amounts of chocolate, he never puts on weight.

   spite

   Tom never puts on weight .... large amounts of chocolate.

40   My grandmother had to sell her house in order to pay off all her debts.

   that

   My grandmother had to sell her house .... pay off all her debts.

For Questions **41–55**, read the text below and look carefully at each line. Some of the lines are correct, and some have a word which should not be there.

If a line is correct, put a tick (✔) by the number **on the separate answer sheet**. If a line has a word which should not be there, write the word **on the separate answer sheet**. There are examples at the beginning (**0** and **00**).

Examples:	0	✔
	00	*to*

0	....	I am writing to tell you what happened when I
00	....	visited to you last week. You will remember that I
41	....	left off your house at about eight as I wanted
42	....	to catch the ten o'clock time train back home. Instead
43	....	of following your advice for to take a bus, I walked to the
44	....	station. I had been walking for twenty minutes when then
45	....	I realised I would not catch the train if I didn't
46	....	hurry up. I started walking more faster and kept looking
47	....	back in case of a bus came. But there wasn't a single
48	....	bus to be seen on the road. Then I did something
49	....	that was so much silly: I decided to go a quicker
50	....	way by cutting myself across the fields, something I
51	....	am used to be doing when I go on holiday. By the time
52	....	I reached the station, the train had been gone, however.
53	....	What is the worse, I had to sleep on a hard bench
54	....	because there wasn't going another train till the following
55	....	day. Some people never follow good advice!

For Questions **56–65**, read the text below. Use the word given in capitals at the end of each line to form a word that fits in the space in the same line. There is an example at the beginning (**0**). Write your answers **on the separate answer sheet**.

Example:	**0**	*ambitious*

MUSIC IN SCHOOLS

Primary schools in London are trying out an (**0**) .*ambitious*. plan   **AMBITION**
through which young children get an (**56**) .... to serious music.   **INTRODUCE**
The idea comes from a group of famous (**57**) .... who are   **MUSIC**
concerned about the (**58**) .... of certain types of classical   **SURVIVE**
music. They see the plan as one possible (**59**) .... to the   **SOLVE**
problem of declining audiences at classical concerts.

Their (**60**) .... is that an interest in classical music should be   **ARGUE**
developed in early (**61**) .... They reject the idea that children   **CHILD**
are (**62**) .... in serious music or necessarily find it boring. The   **INTEREST**
group goes into a school and gives a live (**63**) .... of a short   **PERFORM**
classical piece and then this is followed by an (**64**) .... of how   **EXPLAIN**
the instruments work. These sessions have proved so (**65**) ....   **SUCCESS**
that they have now become a regular feature in some schools.

PAPER 4   Listening (40 minutes)

PART 1   You will hear people talking in eight different situations. For Questions **1–8**, choose the best answer **A**, **B** or **C**.

---

1   You hear part of a play on the radio.
Where is the scene taking place?
  A   in a station
  B   in a shop
  C   in a restaurant

    1

2   You hear a man talking on the telephone.
Who is he talking to?
  A   his boss
  B   his doctor
  C   his teacher

    2

3   You hear a man talking about a car he has hired.
What is his opinion of the car?
  A   It is too old.
  B   It is too slow.
  C   It is too small.

    3

4   You hear a man talking to a friend about a broken vase.
Who does he blame for breaking it?
  A   himself
  B   his friend
  C   a third person

    4

5   You hear a woman talking about something she saw when she was driving.
How did she feel about what she saw?
  A   amused
  B   anxious
  C   angry

    5

6   You hear a woman recommending a hotel.
Why does she recommend the Dorian Hotel?
  A   It is close to tourist attractions.
  B   There are good views to enjoy.
  C   The rooms are very comfortable.

    6

7   You hear the beginning of a radio programme.
What is the radio programme going to be about?
  A   flowers which you can eat
  B   how to grow your own food
  C   becoming a vegetarian

    7

8   You hear a woman talking about a college.
What is her connection with the college?
  A   She is a student there.
  B   She is one of the teachers.
  C   She works as a secretary there.

    8

You will hear part of a wildlife programme which is about birds called waxwings. For Questions **9–18**, complete the sentences.

The interview takes place in a [_____ **9**] in a small town.

The main part of the waxwing's body is [_____ *and* _____ **10**] in colour.

The black marks on the bird's [_____ **11**] are particularly beautiful.

Waxwings usually live in the [_____ **12**] of Europe.

The birds have probably come to England as a result of

[_____ **13**] in their home area.

The time of year when these birds normally come to England is

[_____ **14**]

The food that the birds most like to eat is [_____ **15**]

Many people in the area have reported seeing waxwings in their

[_____ **16**]

One good way of attracting waxwings is to hang [_____ **17**]

from a tree.

The call of a waxwing is said to sound like the noise made by

[_____ **18**]

You will hear five people saying why they like reading novels. For Questions **19–23**, choose from the list **A–F** what each speaker says. Use the letters only once. There is one extra letter which you do not need to use.

Why do you like reading novels?

A   Novels are good for improving language skills.

B   Novels make me forget my problems.

C   Novels add some adventure to my life.

D   Novels are a good subject of conversation.

E   Novels teach me how to act in certain situations.

F   Novels increase my knowledge of other cultures.

Speaker 1		19
Speaker 2		20
Speaker 3		21
Speaker 4		22
Speaker 5		23

You will hear two people talking about holidays. For Questions **24–30**, decide which of the views are expressed by either of the speakers and which are not. In the boxes provided, write **YES** next to those views which are expressed and **NO** next to those views which are not expressed.

24	I generally prefer not to travel abroad on holiday.	24
25	My recent holiday came at an inconvenient moment.	25
26	I once went on a free holiday as a result of my job.	26
27	On holiday, I prefer to choose the activities I take part in.	27
28	Sitting on a beach is enjoyable if you go well-prepared.	28
29	I begin to feel restless if I sit alone in the sun for too long.	29
30	If I have a good book to read, I don't mind where I sit.	30

PAPER 5   Speaking (14 minutes)

P A R T   1   (3 minutes)

Answer these questions:

What type of things do you like to read?
Do you prefer to read a novel or see the film? Why?
Which film actor or actress do you like most? Why?
Do you prefer going to the cinema or watching a video at home? Why?

P A R T   2   (3 or 4 minutes)

Getting away from it all (compare, contrast and speculate)

Turn to pictures 1 and 2 on page 166 which show people enjoying a break from city life.

Candidate A, compare and contrast these photographs, and say why you think the people have chosen to travel in this way. You have a minute to do this.

Candidate B, do you like to get away from it all sometimes?

Clothes (compare, contrast and speculate)

Turn to pictures 1 and 2 on page 167 which show people wearing special clothes.

Candidate B, compare and contrast these photographs, and say why you think the people are wearing these clothes. You have a minute to do this.

Candidate A, are you interested in clothes?

P A R T   3   (3 or 4 minutes)

Electricity (discuss and evaluate)

Turn to the pictures on page 168 which show the different uses of electricity. Imagine that you have to give a talk to young children about the importance of electricity in our lives.

How important is electricity for each of these activities? Which examples would you talk about with a group of young children?

P A R T   4   (3 or 4 minutes)

Answer these questions:

Would you be able to live without electricity? What would you miss most?
Are there any alternatives to the use of electricity?
Which do you think is the best way of making electricity?
How important is it for young children to understand about the environment?
Do the electrical goods we use in the home make us lazy?
How can we help young children to understand what life was like in the past?

TEST 7

PART 1

You are going to read an article about a couple who run a business from their farm in the north of England. Choose the most suitable heading from the list **A–I** for each part (**1–7**) of the article. There is one extra heading which you do not need to use. There is an example at the beginning (**0**).

Mark your answers **on the separate answer sheet**.

A	Professional skills are exploited		**F**	Continuing investment in high standards
B	Ensuring that nothing gets wasted		**G**	Professional recognition is obtained
C	No shortage of ideas to come		**H**	Filling a gap in the market
D	A necessary alternative to farming		**I**	The idea that began it all
E	Time well spent is rewarded			

Waste Not, Want Not

A farming couple who hated to waste misshapen vegetables, have found a profitable way to put them to good use.

0 | **I** |

Bob and Clara Darlington, who own and run a farm in the North of England have always looked for new ways of making money out of the produce they grow. Their success began when they established a shop on their farm, so that people could come and buy fresh vegetables directly from them.

1

The business was an immediate success, and soon scored top marks in a competition set up by the Farm Retail Association to find the best farm shop in the country. The Association's inspectors found the Darlingtons' shop offered excellent service and value for money as well as quality fruit and vegetables.

2

Clara Darlington is a trained chef and, in addition to a range of home-grown foods and other local produce, she began offering a variety of prepared meals which she had made herself in the farmhouse kitchen. A small cafe alongside the farm shop was soon added, with everything that visitors could taste on the menu also being for sale in the shop.

3

Clara admits that starting the business was expensive, and she has worked very hard, but maintains that if the product is good, the public recognise this and buy it. 'I aim to offer the highest quality to our customers, whether they come in for a loaf of bread, or take a whole dinner-party menu. I take it as a compliment if people take home one of my dishes to serve to their family and friends and get away with pretending they made it themselves.'

4

So it was that the couple realised that they had a surplus of misshapen or damaged vegetables grown on the farm which were unsuitable for selling in the shop. Clara, not wishing to see them get thrown away, decided to turn them into soup.

5

The soup met with the immediate approval of customers to the shop and Clara now produces ten different varieties. She spent much of the summer travelling up and down to London by rail, doing presentations of the soups. As a result, they are now served in first-class railway restaurant cars belonging to three companies as well as being stocked by a number of high-class London stores.

6

'I realised there was a huge untapped demand in London and other big cities,' says Clara. 'Because people coming home late from the office find a tub of fresh soup and a slice of bread a quick and tasty easy-to-prepare meal, much healthier than a take-away.'

7

Clara's next idea is to produce a range of pasta sauces handmade to the same standards using natural ingredients and flavours. These she thinks she might be able to sell effectively through mail order. One thing you can be sure of at the Darlingtons' farm, there's always something new going on.

You are going to read an article about a man who has broken a long-distance windsurfing record. For Questions **8–14**, choose the correct answer **A**, **B**, **C** or **D**.

Mark your answers **on the separate answer sheet**.

Windsurfing around Britain

Kevin Cookson, a 23-year-old engineering student, has been keen on windsurfing for many years. Recently, he set a new record for travelling all the way round the coast of Great Britain on a windsurf board.

'I don't really know why I did it,' says Kevin, 'just for the fun of it, I suppose. It was there to be done, that was all.' Despite lacking both the obsessive ambition and the funds that normally go with attempts to break records, Kevin made the journey in eight weeks and six days, knocking one week off the previous record set in 1984.

Leaving from Exmouth in the south-west of England, Kevin travelled up the west coast of England and Wales, before going round the top of Scotland and then coming back down the other side. The journey officially covered 2,896 kilometres, although given the changes of direction to find the right wind paths, the actual distance Kevin travelled is probably closer to 4,000 kilometres.

Kevin fitted his fitness training in around his final year university examinations. 'I didn't have that much time to prepare,' he explains. 'But I went running often and supplemented that with trips to the gym to do weight training. I found I got a lot better during the trip itself actually. At the start, I was tired and needed a rest after four hours, but by the end I found I could do ten hours in a row no trouble.'

Kevin had a budget of £7,000 to cover the whole expedition. The previous record had been set with a budget twice that size, while a recent unsuccessful attempt had cost £40,000. Budgets have to meet the cost of fuel, food and accommodation for the support team, as well as the windsurfer's own equipment and expenses.

Previous contenders had been accompanied by a boat on which they slept at night, as well as a fleet of vehicles on land to carry their supplies. Kevin made do with an inflatable rubber boat and an old van manned by four friends who followed his progress. Overnight arrangements had to be found along the way. Apart from the odd occasion when they enjoyed the hospitality of friends, the team made use of the camping equipment carried in the van, and slept on the beach.

When asked if his athlete's diet was a closely kept secret, Kevin replied that he ate a lot of pasta and relied on the odd tin of tuna to keep up his energy. 'Basically, we had anything that was on special offer in the nearest supermarket,' he confided.

65 Such a prolonged period of **gruelling** windsurfing made relaxation important however, and for this, Kevin favoured the pub method. This also provided social opportunities. 'The people we met were really encouraging,' he recalls. 'They thought what we were doing was really great. It was hard work, but we had a lot of fun along the way.'

Kevin has been windsurfing since he was thirteen years old and is also a highly-ranked competitor at national level. 'I don't know where I'm ranked now,' he says, 'because I've missed a lot of important competitions this year. But what I did has more than made up for that and I'll be doing my best to be up there amongst the winners once I get back into the competitive sport next season.' Given his unique achievement this year, Kevin seems well-placed to take on the world's top windsurfers.

8 Why did Kevin decide to try and break the record?

    A He enjoyed the challenge.
    B It had always been his ambition.
    C It was a way of making money.
    D He was invited to do it by others.

9 Before making the trip, Kevin

    A spent a lot of time practising on water.
    B could already windsurf all day without a break.
    C had only a limited amount of time for training.
    D spent most of his time working out in a gym.

10 How was Kevin's trip unlike earlier attempts at the record?

    A He had no support team.
    B He used better equipment.
    C Only one vehicle was used.
    D It took less time to organise.

11 Where did Kevin sleep most of the time?

    A on a boat
    B in a tent
    C in the van
    D in friends' houses

12 What does Kevin say about his diet?

    A He didn't keep to his plan.
    B Variety was important.
    C Certain foods were essential.
    D It was largely left to chance.

13 What does 'gruelling' (line 65) mean?

    A extremely fast
    B quite lonely
    C very tiring
    D highly uncomfortable

14 How does Kevin feel about regular windsurfing competitions?

    A They no longer interest him.
    B He's sure he can do well in them.
    C He regrets missing them.
    D He has no plans to enter any.

You are going to read a newspaper article about a man who went on a holiday in Canada. Six paragraphs have been removed from the article. Choose from the paragraphs **A–H** the one which fits each gap (**15–20**). There is one extra paragraph which you do not need to use. There is an example at the beginning (**0**).

Mark your answers **on the separate answer sheet**.

All I had to protect me was a leaflet

It was just a leaflet, but it seriously affected my holiday. I had picked it up while innocently looking through a rack of tourist information in Jasper, a city in the Rocky Mountains of Canada.

| 0 | H |

Bears hadn't really figured in my traveller's dreams, but they did that night. 'If you meet a bear, stay calm, talk quietly, don't run,' the leaflet continued. If it was a black bear, all I had to do was play dead, whereas if it was a grizzly, then it was essential that I didn't play dead.

| 15 | |

To find out which of these was best, I asked around. 'I always hum *You are my sunshine*', said a jolly American. 'I just jangle my keys at the corners,' said a local. Many walkers appear to take strap-on bells but these, I was warned, may not be loud enough to do the trick.

| 16 | |

Within ten minutes, in fact, the mighty pine trees were blocking out the daylight, making civilisation seem a distant memory. Somewhere out there, I knew, there were bears. Although I didn't feel that brave, I walked on.

| 17 | |

Yet here I was in a Niagara of sweat as I walked deeper into the forest. There were strange rustlings everywhere. I knew it was time to start singing. I tried some Neil Young. Wasn't he Canadian?

| 18 | |

'The last one was in 1992,' explained a local guide I bumped into. 'It was a guy who went camping up in the backwoods.' And then he added: 'He was British too.'

| 19 | |

'Of course, it's the elks that are really dangerous at this time of year,' he let slip. 'What you mean the ones wandering all over town?' I replied. 'Sure you've got to keep well away from them when they're calving, they've got hooves like razors.'

| 20 | |

But don't be discouraged from visiting Jasper. The mountains are lovely and you get a great view from the Tour bus, or the local tramway that climbs up to 8200 feet. And neither of these attractions is patronised by bears!

A I had experienced similar fears on walking safaris in Africa. Except that there you do it in the company of a trained guide with a big gun. All you get for protection in Canada is a leaflet. Canada, I complained to the lonely trees, is supposed to be safe and calm, that's why people go there.

B Fortunately, May is one of the best months to see bears, I was informed. This was confirmed by a list of that week's sightings posted to the notice board in the park's Information Centre.

C Well, I'm glad to say I completed my hike without being attacked by either animal. But I can't say that I enjoyed it, I was too terrified for that.

D The thing is, and this is no joke, people do, very very rarely, get attacked by bears. As many as five visitors have died from bear-related incidents since the park opened in 1907.

E So I decided to trust to my own voice. Armed with nothing but a map, an apple, and a bottle of water, I set off on a three-hour hike. It was only a few kilometres out of the city, but to a timid townsperson like myself, it seemed wild enough.

F All of a sudden, the prospect of walking alone in the Canadian woods didn't seem so attractive. At breakfast, I reread the leaflet very carefully. It was important not to surprise a bear. To avoid this one should whistle, talk, sing or carry a noise maker.

G This comment really made my day. But he went on to tell me that only five percent of visitors to the Jasper National Park ever get to see a bear.

H 'You're in wild bear country,' it warned, and there were graphic pictures of both black bears and grizzly bears. I had come to Jasper to go walking in the mountains. I had a vision of enjoying the snowy peaks, mystic forests, and soothing lakes.

You are going to read a magazine article in which four men talk about the clothes they like to wear. For Questions **21–35**, choose from the people (**A–D**). The people may be chosen more than once. There is an example at the beginning (**0**).

Mark your answers **on the separate answer sheet**.

Which of the men

sometimes tries to surprise people through the clothes he wears?	**0**	*D*
admits that his clothes are generally untidy?	**21**	
buys clothes which last a long time?	**22**	
is used to being criticised for the clothes he chooses?	**23**	
likes to get a good deal when buying clothes?	**24**	
needs help with clothes for less formal occasions?	**25**	
needs to have the right clothes to get work?	**26**	
needs help in choosing his clothes?	**27**	
needs different clothes for different types of work?	**28**	
admits he doesn't look after his clothes very well?	**29**	
prefers to take his time when choosing clothes?	**30**	
relies on personal judgement when choosing what to wear?	**31**	
tends to avoid clothes in bright colours?	**32**	
used to work in a job where clothes were provided?	**33**	
wants to change his appearance completely?	**34**	
wants to buy clothes which are suitable for his age?	**35**	

You are what you wear

Four men talk about what they wear and why

A — Alan Upshire

I would like to be taller. I have a long body and short legs, but I have no problems in dressing for work – smart suits, shirts and ties are the order of the day, and I do invest in good quality suits that keep going for years. My appearance is important for the work I do and I now know what labels to buy for suits that are going to fit well. What I have trouble with is casual wear for weekends – you know, the right sort of informal look for supper with friends, or taking the kids out. I'd like to find the perfect casual jacket, but I hate ties and wouldn't wear one out of work. I want to look casual and stylish even though I'm in my forties. I don't like to see older men wearing trainers, but I don't know what type of casual shoes to buy, for example.

B — Barry Sheldon

Being an actor, the way I look can affect my opportunities and the parts I get. I've got used to wearing my hair long, but I know it's time for a change now. But how short do I go, and what style should I choose? That's the problem because I want it to look dramatic, I want a new look. My style of dressing is simple and stylish, especially for rehearsals when I'll go in jeans and T-shirt. But I also work part-time at a film-sales company and, although I work mostly on the telephone, I have to look smarter. I don't mind shopping for clothes, but I'm not very good if I have anyone with me because I like to browse at my own pace, you know, try lots of things on. I find I buy a lot of things in black and white. It's simple and stylish and easy to put together.

C — Chris Theydon

I hate shopping for clothes and will only do so when it's absolutely necessary – about once every six months. My girlfriend usually comes with me because she has better taste than I do! I'd describe my style of dress as very casual, perhaps bordering on scruffy. I try to avoid wearing smart clothes, and this may be something to do with the fact that I'm hopeless at keeping things smart. Ironing's a skill I've never really mastered, for example. Also, as I was in uniform for about twelve years when I was in the army, I never really had to think about all this somehow. I know I should be smarter for work, but it's a pretty relaxed office and so jeans and T-shirt is the norm. It's very rare for me to wear a suit, but as I've got about three friends' weddings coming up, perhaps I ought to think about a new one.

D — Des Waltham

I would describe my style of dressing as individual. I know what I like and I know what will suit a particular occasion. I'm very worried about the effect clothes have on the way other people react to you. I'll wear a suit if I think it will make a meeting more productive or my oldest jeans if I want to shock people. I like shopping and I like clothes, but I don't like shopping for clothes. Where I shop depends on where I am and as I travel abroad a lot, I'm also looking for bargains in the sales wherever I go. One problem is that my wife is a fashion designer and so I always get a reaction to the things I buy, although she's long since given up trying to influence me.

PART 1

You **must** answer this question.

1 You have seen an advertisement for volunteers in an Environmental Improvement Project in your area. You want to offer your help during the summer holidays but you need to know more. Using the notes you have made, write to the Environmental Improvement Project giving relevant details **and** asking for further information.

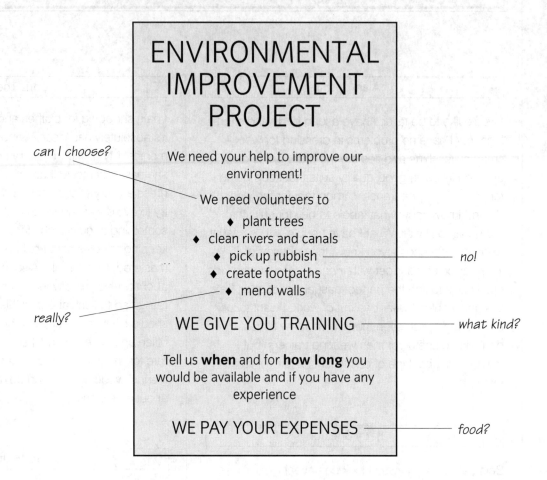

can I choose?

ENVIRONMENTAL IMPROVEMENT PROJECT

We need your help to improve our environment!

We need volunteers to

- ◆ plant trees
- ◆ clean rivers and canals
- ◆ pick up rubbish   *no!*
- ◆ create footpaths
- ◆ mend walls

really?

WE GIVE YOU TRAINING   *what kind?*

Tell us **when** and for **how long** you would be available and if you have any experience

WE PAY YOUR EXPENSES   *food?*

Write a **letter** of between **120** and **180** words in an appropriate style. Do not write any addresses.

Write an answer to **one** of the Questions **2–5** in this part. Write your answer in **120–180** words in an appropriate style.

2   Your class recently had a discussion about the importance of exercise and sport for keeping fit. Your teacher has now asked you to write a composition giving your opinion on the subject. This is the title of the composition.

Which is the best way for young people to keep fit; working out in a gym or playing a team sport?

Write your **composition**.

3   You have decided to enter a short story competition organised by an international magazine. The short story should begin with these words:

It was the last day of the summer holidays and I wasn't expecting much to happen …

Write your **story**.

4   Your school is planning to start a video club showing films in English. As a member of the committee, you have been asked to write a report suggesting the different types of film the club should show to appeal to as many students in the school as possible.

Write your **report**.

5   Answer **one** of the following two questions based on your reading of **one** of the set books.

Either   (a) A penfriend in another country who also studies English has asked you to recommend a book to read in the summer holidays. Write to your friend saying whether the book you have read would be a good choice.

Write your **letter**. Do not include any addresses.

Or   (b) Your teacher wants to read a short passage from the book you have read to a class of younger students. She aims to give them an idea of what the book is like and encourage them to read it. She has asked you to write a report saying which passage from the book would be most suitable and why.

Write your **report**.

Use of English (1 hour 15 minutes)

For Questions **1–15**, read the text below and decide which answer **A, B, C** or **D** best fits each space. There is an example at the beginning (**0**).

Mark your answers **on the separate answer sheet**.

Example:

0 **A** took   **B** made   **C** went   **D** left

0	A	B	C	D
	▆	☐	☐	☐

THE FLYING AUNTIES

Few passengers on the British Airways flight to Hong Kong which (**0**) ..... off from London Airport on Saturday 7th August, were (**1**) ..... that their flight was setting a record for the company. In fact their plane was carrying 112 'unaccompanied minors' – the largest (**2**) ..... of children travelling without parents or guardians ever to have flown on a (**3**) ..... flight. Most of these children, aged from six (**4**) ....., were returning to Hong Kong after taking three-week English (**5**) ..... at various language schools as (**6**) ..... an exchange scheme.

The children were not left to their own devices, (**7**) ...... Airline rules say that children under twelve can only fly if accompanied (**8**) ..... an adult. So, a group of three 'aunties' and one 'uncle' flew with them to (**9**) ..... them entertained and (**10**) ..... with any problems that might arise. They are part of a British Airways team known as the 'flying aunties'. These are BA employees who volunteer, in their own time, to (**11**) ..... an escorted service for unaccompanied minors to both European and long-haul (**12**) ...... Once in the air, there is a range of activities available to the youngsters (**13**) ..... computer games, colouring books and soft drinks on tap. In (**14**) ....., the children have the 'aunties' all to themselves – for such members of (**15**) ..... do not take on other duties.

1	**A**	realised	**B**	thought	**C**	aware	**D**	known
2	**A**	count	**B**	amount	**C**	number	**D**	quantity
3	**A**	unique	**B**	solo	**C**	single	**D**	lone
4	**A**	upwards	**B**	forwards	**C**	afterwards	**D**	backwards
5	**A**	classes	**B**	courses	**C**	studies	**D**	lessons
6	**A**	linked to	**B**	long as	**C**	part of	**D**	along with
7	**A**	however	**B**	although	**C**	altogether	**D**	moreover
8	**A**	from	**B**	by	**C**	with	**D**	at
9	**A**	hold	**B**	get	**C**	help	**D**	keep
10	**A**	manage	**B**	deal	**C**	solve	**D**	bother
11	**A**	provide	**B**	produce	**C**	pretend	**D**	present
12	**A**	departures	**B**	routes	**C**	destinations	**D**	arrivals
13	**A**	regarding	**B**	composing	**C**	containing	**D**	including
14	**A**	further	**B**	addition	**C**	extra	**D**	plus
15	**A**	staff	**B**	crew	**C**	team	**D**	group

For Questions **16–30**, read the text below and think of the word which best fits each space. Use only **one** word in each space. There is an example at the beginning (**0**).

Write your answers **on the separate answer sheet**.

Example:	**0**	*one*

LIQUORICE ALLSORTS

Bassett's Liquorice Allsorts have been (**0**) .... of Britain's favourite sweets for more (**16**) .... a hundred years. Each box contains a selection of the eight different liquorice sweets, each of (**17**) .... has a name. On the box itself is a picture of Bertie Bassett, a figure (**18**) .... body is made entirely from Allsorts. Over forty million Allsorts are now produced every week at the company's plant (**19**) .... the city of Sheffield and these are exported all (**20**) .... the world.

Yet the idea for the product was the result (**21**) .... an accident. In June 1899, Bassett's was already selling the individual liquorice sweets separately, when company employee, Charlie Thompson, dropped a tray full of them (**22**) .... a presentation to the owner of a sweet shop. Seeing (**23**) .... good they looked all mixed (**24**) .... on the floor, the shop owner said he (**25**) .... like to sell the sweets, (**26**) .... only if they could be sold as a mixture.

A new brand (**27**) .... thus created which soon became very popular. It has been in production (**28**) .... since. For something created purely (**29**) .... chance, the success of the product has been incredible. (**30**) .... its rather old-fashioned image, it is one of those brands which continues to grow, according to reports issued by the sweet industry.

For Questions **31–40**, complete the second sentence so that it has a similar meaning to the first sentence, using the word given. **Do not change the word given.** You must use between two and five words, including the word given. Here is an example (**0**).

Example: **0** Clara started to understand mathematics better after she'd changed school.

understanding

Clara's .... to improve after she'd changed school.

The gap can be filled by the words 'understanding of mathematics started' so you write:

0	*understanding of mathematics started*

Write **only the missing words** on the separate answer sheet.

---

31 Nigel asked if Ann could lend him her hairdryer for a while.

borrow

Nigel asked .... hairdryer for a while.

32 Chris is hungry because the last time he ate anything was Thursday evening.

not

Chris is hungry because he .... Thursday evening.

33 We will not be able to solve this difficult problem.

impossible

It will be .... a solution to this difficult problem.

34 Peter is angry because Joanna did not accept his invitation.

turned

If Joanna .... his invitation, Peter wouldn't be angry.

35 I don't think I can manage if Sheila doesn't help me.

do

I think I can't .... help.

36 'Have you finished your homework yet?' Mr Brown asked his daughter.

if

Mr Brown asked his daughter .... homework yet.

37 'Do we have to pay for our own tickets?' I asked my friend.

expected

I asked my friend .... pay for our own tickets.

38 The strong winds caused the tower to fall over.

knocked

It was the strong winds .... over.

39 The bus driver stopped frequently to allow the tourists to see the sights.

that

The bus driver stopped frequently .... see the sights.

40 Martha held George's hand and prevented him from falling over.

had

George would have fallen over .... his hand.

For Questions **41–55**, read the text below and look carefully at each line. Some of the lines are correct, and some have a word which should not be there.

If a line is correct, put a tick (✔) by the number **on the separate answer sheet**. If a line has a word which should not be there, write the word **on the separate answer sheet**. There are examples at the beginning (**0** and **00**).

Examples:	0	*for*
	00	✔

0	....	As you were not able to come to London for to see
00	....	the open-air concert, I am sure you are looking
41	....	forward to be hearing all about it from me.
42	....	I am sorry that to have to disappoint you, but the truth
43	....	is that I did also watched it on television. As you
44	....	know, I bought my ticket months ago because
45	....	I knew they would be sold out of very quickly.
46	....	Let me tell you what has happened that day. I wanted
47	....	to be one of the first person to arrive at the concert hall
48	....	to get a good seat right in front, near from the stage,
49	....	so I took up an early train. But when I got there, I realised
50	....	that I had left my ticket at home. So I had to go all the way
51	....	back to get it, which it took at least an hour. But then,
52	....	believe it or not, the organisers would not let me in because
53	....	the concert had already started! I was so much angry with
54	....	them. They simply refused to listen to my explanations.
55	....	In the end, I went back to home and switched on the TV!

For Questions **56–65**, read the text below. Use the word given in capitals at the end of each line to form a word that fits in the space in the same line. There is an example at the beginning (**0**). Write your answers **on the separate answer sheet**.

Example:	0	*fascination*

THE WILD WEST

In the USA, people have a (**0**) *fascination* for everything connected   **FASCINATE**
with the 'wild west' of the cowboy era. This has led to (**56**) ....   **VARY**
activities which are of interest to (**57**) .... who are travelling   **TOUR**
around the western states. There are (**58**) .... of wild west painting,   **EXHIBIT**
concerts of cowboy music and, most (**59**) .... of all, live rodeo   **EXCITE**
shows to watch.

Rodeos, where cowboys take part in horse-riding (**60**) .... for big   **COMPETE**
money prizes, are (**61**) .... popular. There are 739 each year, held   **EXTREME**
in giant (**62**) .... arenas as well as open-air show grounds across   **DOOR**
the west. Most of the riders are professional (**63**) ...., but most of   **PERFORM**
the events were (**64**) .... based on the cowboys' everyday working   **ORIGIN**
tasks. Despite some concerns over possible (**65**) .... to horses,   **CRUEL**
most people are thrilled by the display of skill and daring to be seen at a
rodeo.

PAPER 4   Listening (40 minutes)

PART 1 You will hear people talking in eight different situations. For Questions **1–8**, choose the best answer **A**, **B** or **C**.

1 You hear part of a news report about complaints against railway companies.
   What does David Driver think about the situation?
   A The railway companies are doing their best.
   B The situation has improved slightly.
   C The complaints are exaggerated.

   `[ ]` 1

2 On a phone-in consumer programme, you hear a call from a listener.
   What is she doing when she speaks?
   A explaining why a mistake occurred
   B justifying her behaviour
   C asking for advice

   `[ ]` 2

3 You hear a man talking about a campaign he has been organising.
   What is the aim of the campaign?
   A to influence a decision that will be taken
   B to support a decision that has been taken
   C to prevent a decision being taken at the moment

   `[ ]` 3

4 You hear part of an interview with a woman who used to run an agency for photographic models. Why did she give up the business?
   A It became too big.
   B She wanted to sell it.
   C It no longer interested her.

   `[ ]` 4

5 You hear an announcement about library services.
   How are the services going to change?
   A the number of staff employed
   B the way money is collected
   C the times when they are available

   `[ ]` 5

6 You hear part of an interview with a famous writer.
   What is his attitude towards ideas?
   A Old ideas can always be recycled.
   B Unused ideas may be useful one day.
   C There is no such thing as a new idea.

   `[ ]` 6

7 You hear a woman talking about an artist.
   What is her opinion of the artist?
   A She admires his courage.
   B She respects his commitment.
   C She appreciates his difficulties.

   `[ ]` 7

8 You hear part of a radio phone-in programme.
   What type of advice is the caller asking for?
   A how to repair something
   B how to find something he needs
   C how to change the appearance of something

   `[ ]` 8

You will hear part of a wildlife programme about a snake which comes from a group of islands in the Caribbean. For Questions **9–18**, complete the sentences.

The racer snake is one of the [_____ **9**] snakes in the world.

It is thought that around [_____ **10**] wild racer snakes are living in the Caribbean area.

Martin describes the news about racer snakes as [_____ **11**]

By last autumn, [_____ **12**] had been produced at the Wildlife Trust in Britain.

Martin describes baby racer snakes as too [____ *and* ____ **13**] to handle.

There are plans to set up a [_____ **14**] on an island in the Caribbean.

A group has been formed on the island to educate both

[_____ *and* ____ **15**] about the wildlife.

A leading researcher now has the job of [_____ **16**] the racer snakes on the island.

Racer snakes on the island were being attacked by both

[_____ **17**] and the mongoose.

You can tell when a racer snake has been attacked because of the

[_____ **18**] marks on its body.

PART 3

You will hear five students who want a summer job in an office saying why they are suitable for the job. For Questions **19–23**, choose from the list **A–F** what each speaker says. Use the letters only once. There is one extra letter which you do not need to use.

A   I have had work experience.

B   I have worked on projects.

C   I work well in teams.

D   I have a good grasp of written language.

E   I pay attention to detail.

F   I know the company well.

Speaker 1 [   ] **19**

Speaker 2 [   ] **20**

Speaker 3 [   ] **21**

Speaker 4 [   ] **22**

Speaker 5 [   ] **23**

PART 4

You will hear a radio interview with Dominic Austin, a science-fiction writer. For Questions **24–30**, choose the best answer **A**, **B** or **C**.

24   What reason did one firm of publishers give for not accepting Dominic's first book?
  A   its subject
  B   its style
  C   its length

[   ] **24**

25   Dominic wanted the characters in his books
  A   to be as realistic as possible.
  B   to change as the story developed.
  C   to be likeable people.

[   ] **25**

26   What happens when Dominic writes a good series of books?
  A   Readers want more of the same.
  B   He gets tired of receiving letters.
  C   Many publishers offer him contracts.

[   ] **26**

27   What is Dominic's ambition at the moment?
  A   to win an award in the science-fiction field
  B   to get more people to read his novels
  C   to improve his story-telling skills

[   ] **27**

28   Dominic says that he accepted a film offer because
  A   he was too proud to reject it.
  B   he was promised high earnings.
  C   he wanted a rest from writing.

[   ] **28**

29   As a young child Dominic enjoyed reading
  A   poems.
  B   fictional stories.
  C   books about history.

[   ] **29**

30   What does Dominic say readers should do before buying a book?
  A   read reviews of the book
  B   read a small section of it
  C   find out about the author

[   ] **30**

PAPER 5   **Speaking** (14 minutes)

Answer these questions:

Tell us about the type of food you like to eat.
Do you prefer eating at home or eating out?
Who cooks most of the food you eat?
Do you prefer formal meals or informal snacks?

Classrooms (compare and contrast)

Turn to pictures 1 and 2 on page 169 which show different classrooms.

Candidate A, compare and contrast these photographs, and say which of the classrooms is better organised. You have a minute to do this.

Candidate B, which of these classrooms do you prefer?

Food shops (compare and contrast)

Turn to pictures 1 and 2 on page 170 which show different kinds of shops where you can buy food.

Candidate B, compare and contrast these photographs, and say which type of shop provides a better service. You have a minute to do this.

Candidate A, which of these shops would you rather buy food from?

A long weekend (discuss and evaluate)

Turn to the pictures on page 171 which show different weekend activities. Imagine that a group of students from another country is coming to spend a long weekend in your area to learn about the local culture.

What type of places should they visit? Which activities should they do? Plan their weekend timetable.

Answer these questions:

How important is it to understand the culture of other countries?
Which country would you choose to visit if you could?
Apart from exchange visits, how else can we share our culture with others?
How difficult do you think it would be to live in another country?

TEST 8

PAPER 1   Reading (1 hour 15 minutes)

PART 1 You are going to read an extract from an article about a businesswoman. Choose from the list **A–I** the sentence which best summarises each part (**1–7**) of the extract. There is one extra sentence which you do not need to use. There is an example at the beginning (**0**).

Mark your answers **on the separate answer sheet**.

A   An up-market product

B   Attracted to her latest interests

C   Facing up to competition

D   Building a range of colours

E   Initial involvement pays off

F   Personal taste influences a decision

G   Building on previous success

H   The thinking behind a decision

I   An unusual combination of interests

THE LADY WITH BLUE NAILS

Sandy Lerner is founder of an unusual range of nail-polish colours

0   *I*

The links between computers and cosmetics are not obvious, but one of the most successful self-made businesswomen in the USA, Sandy Lerner, has made her fortune in both.

1

With her long purple hair and taste for blue nail polish, it is not surprising that Sandy got fed up with not being able to find make-up she liked. After a brief spell of mixing her own colours, Sandy decided to set up her own company.

2

Since its launch in 1996, her company has taken the USA, Asia and Europe by storm. 'At the time everyone was still heavily into pinks and reds,' says Sandy, 'and I thought that given other developments going on in the fashion world, the time was ripe for an alternative.'

3

It's one thing to like blue nail polish yourself, but quite another to set up a company making it, however. 'The more money you have, the easier that decision is to make,' she admits. And she has plenty. Sandy made her fortune in a former career as a computer specialist. She set up a company in 1984 after designing a piece of technology which is now used in 80% of connections on the Internet.

4

The new company is proving to be a nice little earner too. As founder and chief executive of the company, Sandy was personally responsible for designing the eye-catching advertising campaigns that helped at the beginning, although she now tends to leave the day-to-day business to her partners.

5

But establishing the business was not easy, particularly when the large cosmetics companies realised there was a market for alternative colours and started selling them too. 'As an alternative, we're never going to threaten the main market of the big companies,' says Sandy, 'and although they now do similar colours, they only do a few of them. So people who want intense and complicated colours will still come to us.'

6

Although shades of blue, purple, yellow and green sound like just the thing for teenage girls and punks, the company actually aims its products at career women in their thirties and forties. Sandy thinks make-up is about a state of mind, 'It's for self-confident people who are not afraid of something you can wash off.' Indeed, the unusual colours and successful marketing campaigns, make the company's products a hit amongst Hollywood celebrities.

7

Although she keeps a close eye on the company, Sandy admits that she quickly loses interest once a project is up and running. She is now turning her attention to her current projects; a large country house in England, her farm in Virginia where she keeps horses and a new project for promoting nineteenth-century literature on the Internet.

You are going to read an article about an actor. For Questions **8–14**, choose the correct answer **A**, **B**, **C** or **D**.

Mark your answers **on the separate answer sheet**.

Thirty-five years ago, Malcolm Burwell was a very successful young actor appearing in a number of series on British television. He was lucky, he'd made it to the top quite quickly and had plenty of work. Hollywood directors had even begun to suggest that he might like to think of making his fortune across the Atlantic. But two things made Malcolm think twice about these offers. He didn't want to move his young family to the USA, and a mystery illness was beginning to throw his whole future into doubt.

Malcolm had a problem with his voice. It began to grow steadily weaker and weaker until hospital treatment became
19 necessary. Before **this** finally took effect, however, he found he could hardly talk. As he remembers, 'When you are in danger of losing something central to your career, it makes you think very hard. I have to say I learnt a lot from the experience.'

'My voice recovered, but it taught me the importance of getting the best out of what you've got. As it got better and stronger, I started doing things like public readings of poetry and pieces of literature, just to use it professionally again.' This turned out to be the start of a whole new direction for his career. So popular have these readings become, that Malcolm is now extremely familiar to people as the voice on a number of readings of best-selling books which have been recorded on to tape. Instantly

recognisable, his voice is now a much
41 **sought-after** commodity.

Malcolm first approached publishers with the idea of selling books on tape all those years ago. At first, they said that only blind people listened to books on tape. But times were changing and when he did eventually convince one of them to try it, instant success followed. Now the market for such tapes in Britain is worth £25 million a year.

Although Malcolm continues to work in television and theatre, it is his readings of literature that have really made his name. When he is recording Malcolm uses his voice to give an impression of the different characters. 'I don't try to convince the audience that I am an 11-year-old boy at one moment and his grandfather the next,' he says, 'but I use my voice to try and make the listener believe that I've really got a story to tell them rather than just a book to read out.'

Malcolm carefully does his homework on any book he has agreed to record, although he knows that some actors do not. He tells the story of one well-known British actor whose enthusiastic producer commented on what a great thriller it was they were about to record. 'Is it?' said the actor, opening the script for the first time. 'Oh good.' All very well, says Malcolm, until you discover on page two hundred that the character you've given a Scottish accent to is supposed to come from Wales!

8 Why did Malcolm not go to the USA thirty-five years ago?

    A   His family opposed it.
    B   The offers weren't good enough.
    C   He was in poor health.
    D   He already had work in Britain.

9 What does 'this' in line 19 refer to?

    A   the treatment he received
    B   the effects of losing his voice
    C   the hospital he went to
    D   the weakness of his voice

10 How did Malcolm's illness affect his career?

    A   He could no longer do certain types of work.
    B   He had to be very careful when using his voice.
    C   It made him appreciate his voice more.
    D   It forced him to look for new areas of work.

11 What does 'sought-after' (line 41) mean?

    A   makes a lot of money
    B   everyone knows it
    C   it cannot be copied
    D   everyone wants it

12 How did publishers react initially to the idea of books on tape?

    A   They thought the market was limited.
    B   They thought nobody would buy them.
    C   They were keen to open up a new market.
    D   They realised it was a good idea.

13 When recording, Malcolm is keen to convince his listeners that

    A   different people are reading the story.
    B   he is actually telling them a story.
    C   the events are really happening.
    D   they are sitting in the theatre.

14 Malcolm relates the story about the other actor in order to show how

    A   good he is.
    B   difficult the job is.
    C   important it is to prepare.
    D   different approaches can work.

You are going to read a magazine article about a man who studies mountain lions in the USA. Seven sentences have been removed from the article. Choose from the sentences **A–I** the one which fits each gap (**15–21**). There is one extra sentence which you do not need to use. There is an example at the beginning (**0**).

Mark your answers **on the separate answer sheet**.

FACE-TO-FACE WITH A MOUNTAIN LION

Something was watching me. I stopped. Not a leaf moved, not a bird called. Then, less than a hundred metres away amongst the trees, I saw him. Just his face, eyes the colour of amber, whiskers glistening in the late afternoon sun.

Felis concolor, or the cat of one colour was the ghost of North America. It has a variety of names such as cougar and puma, but is most commonly known simply as the mountain lion. It was 1965. I was just beginning my life's work of trying to understand these secretive and elusive cats. **0** | *I* |

A few years earlier, following five years of doing research into the habits of grizzly bears with my brother, also a wildlife biologist, I had sought a project of my own. **15**

Mountain lions seemed not only challenging but also romantic. Once they were found across the entire continent. But after centuries of ruthless hunting, they had been confined to a few wild spots. In the early 1960s, mountain lions were still considered as the enemy. Farmers, ranchers and hunters were trying to rid the world of these great cats. **16**

Many colleagues tried to discourage me. The lions moved across hundreds of miles of territory. I would never be able to keep track of them for long enough to study them. Moreover, as most mountain lions live in difficult country, they are best tracked in snow. That meant living in tents in winter and tracking with dogs in the intense cold before trapping them in a tree so that they could be captured and marked. **17**

By capturing and recapturing, and each time making very careful observations, I hoped to build a fund of information about these mysterious animals.

I began in January 1963, marking sixteen lions within a hundred miles of Missoula, Montana. **18** So I moved, next season, as far from civilisation as I could get in the USA, to the Idaho Primitive Area, a roadless wilderness in Salmon River Country.

I hired Wilbur Wiles, the best professional wildcat tracker in Idaho. Still, that winter we could not find enough lions for a valid study. **19** A meaningful study of mountain lions might be impossible. I decided to expand the study area. In the summer of 1965, I backpacked into the wilderness, into new territory.

Then, at the mouth of a small valley, I noticed some footprints. I forced my way through the undergrowth up the narrow valley and suddenly broke into a beautiful mountain meadow ringed by trees. **20**

I don't know how long we stared at each other. It was a wonderful moment. Every other mountain lion I had seen had been up a tree, cornered by the dogs below, or drugged by the tranquillisers we used to mark them in safety. Eventually this lion broke our gaze, turned his head slowly, and with majestic grace, leapt into full view. **21** I can still see his eyes. I've often thought he brought me good luck because that was indeed a turning point. The next winter's work went extremely well.

A   I was beginning to think maybe my colleagues were right.

B   But I was willing to give all that a try.

C   He encouraged me to tackle something tough.

D   It was then that I felt those eyes.

E   Then he was gone.

F   And yet we knew almost nothing about them.

G   These animals are territorial and limit their own numbers.

H   But by the spring, most of those had been shot by hunters.

I   The effort had not been going well.

You are going to read a magazine article in which different people talk about letter writing. For Questions **22–35**, choose from the people (**A–F**). Some of the people may be chosen more than once. When more than one answer is required, these may be given in any order. There is an example at the beginning (**0**).

Mark your answers **on the separate answer sheet**.

A	**Amanda Littleport**
B	**Barbara Lynn**
C	**Charles Downham**
D	**Derek Watlington**
E	**Elizabeth Brandon**
F	**Fiona Stretham**

Which of the people

chooses to write letters for health reasons? **0** *B*

thinks some letters should not be posted? **22**

describes a regular letter-writing routine? **23**

has help with the letters he/she has to write? **24**

compares letter-writing with another activity? **25**

is expected to write letters as part of a job? **26** **27**

has made a point of keeping letters? **28** **29**

is aware of expressing his/her feeling more freely in letters? **30**

feels that electronic aids make letter writing less personal? **31** **32**

writes letters designed to amuse the reader? **33**

takes care over the appearance of their letters? **34** **35**

Just a few lines …

E-mails are easy and faxes are fast – so is the old-fashioned letter really a thing of the past? According to a recent survey, 10% of the 18 billion letters delivered annually in Britain are private ones, so there must be people out there who are sitting down and putting pen to paper in the old-fashioned way.

For example, there's novelist **Amanda Littleport** who says, 'It's a very personal way of keeping in touch. I find I include things in letters that I might not mention in conversation, such as things I don't like about other people for example. But something nice, said in a letter becomes much more special. That's why love letters are so important.' Amanda always writes with a fountain pen. 'What looks best is black ink on pure white paper. A letter is like a gift you give someone, it's upsetting to see a lovely letter on horrible paper.'

The actress **Barbara Lynn**, if she's at home in London, writes at least three letters each morning at a desk in an upstairs bedroom that has become her 'writing room'. 'I find it an enjoyable experience, as important as talking to people. As I am deaf in one ear, I find the telephone difficult, and I don't have e-mail. Letters written by hand are an exchange of energy between people. It's like the energy that passes between an actor and audience in the theatre, which doesn't happen on film or television in the same way.'

Unlike Amanda and Barbara, playwright, **Charles Downham** confesses that he finds letter writing increasingly difficult. 'I never seem to get the time these days. I like receiving them though. I've got a cardboard box of them stored in the attic, so that I can reread them in my old age.' He also chooses his notepaper with care. 'I love wandering around stationery shops. It's something to do with the feel of the quality product. The matching envelope is an absolute must.'

Television Presenter, **Derek Watlington** is a well-known letter writer. He has carried on a 30-year correspondence with his actress wife whenever their work has kept them apart. Fortunately, both parties have held on to the letters, allowing them to be published last year, minus the 'silliest bits'. One of them begins, 'I do miss your letters when we're together ...' and the tone is light-hearted and amusing throughout, even when the subject matter is serious. 'I always hand-write my letters,' he says. 'Even though a word-processor means you can go back and improve things, there's something about the machine that brings out the more formal side of my character, so letters written on one are never quite so intimate.'

Politicians like **Elizabeth Brandon** have headed notepaper provided for them once they get elected to the Houses of Parliament, and there are special desks with old-fashioned dip pens and supplies of real ink for them to use for letter writing. Barbara is a shameless lover of gadgets, however, and prefers to reply to people by dictating letters into a cassette recorder so that her secretary can type them up and fax them. 'But I also write long chatty e-mails to my husband and daughter when I am away,' she says.

Don't even think of mentioning e-mails to **Fiona Stretham**, a journalist who is the 'agony aunt' for a top weekly magazine. Her problem page attracts hundreds of letters, all of which receive a personal reply. She thinks the handwriting is often a real clue to the personality and sincerity of the writer. 'I can't stand e-mail,' she says. 'They're so cold and concise.' She laments the general decline in letter writing as a way of letting off steam. 'Lots of people will remember heartfelt complaints or declarations of love that never got as far as the postbox. The act of just telling someone how you feel makes <u>you</u> feel better, even if <u>they</u> never get to read it!'

So it seems, the letter is not dead. But the thing to remember is that it's a two-way process. As a friend of Groucho Marx once wrote: 'Dear Groucho, I would have answered your letter sooner, but you didn't send one.'

PAPER 2   Writing (1 hour 30 minutes)

You **must** answer this question.

1   You and a group of friends want to spend two days in a new Wildlife Learning and Leisure Centre outside your town. You have a leaflet with details about the centre but you need to know more. Using the notes you have made, write to the centre asking for more information and giving them relevant details.

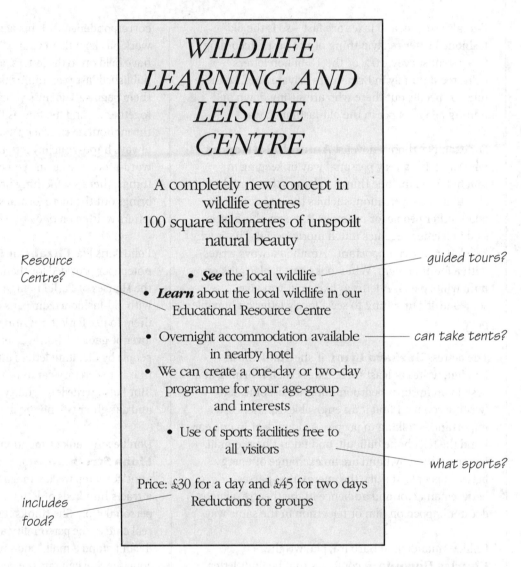

Resource Centre?

guided tours?

can take tents?

what sports?

includes food?

WILDLIFE LEARNING AND LEISURE CENTRE

A completely new concept in wildlife centres
100 square kilometres of unspoilt natural beauty

- **See** the local wildlife
- **Learn** about the local wildlife in our Educational Resource Centre

- Overnight accommodation available in nearby hotel
- We can create a one-day or two-day programme for your age-group and interests

- Use of sports facilities free to all visitors

Price: £30 for a day and £45 for two days
Reductions for groups

Write a **letter** of between **120** and **180** words in an appropriate style. Do not write any addresses.

Write an answer to **one** of the Questions 2–5 in this part. Write your answer in **120–180** words in an appropriate style.

2   You have decided to enter a short-story writing competition. The rules of the competition say that the story must begin with these words:

Looking back on that day, we all agreed it was our greatest victory.

Write your **story**.

3   You have received this letter from an English-speaking penfriend.

> *We're doing a project at college on the fashion industry in different countries. It would be nice to include a first-hand report from someone living abroad. The report should describe how fashions for young people have changed in recent years. Can you help?*

Write your **report**.

4   Following a class discussion on the environment, your teacher has asked you to write a composition with this title:

Some people think the recycling of used glass and paper is a waste of time. Do you agree?

Write your **composition**.

5   Answer **one** of the following two questions based on your reading of **one** of the set books.

Either   (a)   You have seen this announcement in an international magazine for young people.

> *Have you read a good book lately?*
> *We're offering a prize of £200 for the best article recommending a good book to our readers.*

Write your **article**.

Or   (b)   In a review of the book you have read you have seen this comment.

> *'It's difficult to believe in the characters in this story as real people.'*

Your teacher has asked you to write a composition giving your reasons for either agreeing or disagreeing with this comment.

Write your **composition**.

PAPER 3

Use of English (1 hour 15 minutes)

PART 1

For Questions **1–15**, read the text below and decide which answer **A**, **B**, **C** or **D** best fits each space. There is an example at the beginning (**0**).

Mark your answers **on the separate answer sheet**.

Example:

0	**A** up	**B** to	**C** off	**D** with

0	A �in	B ☐	C ☐	D ☐

THE EARTH GALLERIES

To many people the word 'geology' conjures (**0**) ..... rather dull images of lumps of rock in glass cases. People (**1**) ..... to regard geology as an academic subject that you don't need to know about (**2**) ..... you have to study it at school. If you visit the Earth Galleries at London's Natural History Museum, however, you'll (**3**) ..... that this image couldn't be (**4**) ..... from the truth.

The (**5**) ..... of the exhibition is not to produce future geologists, but rather to inspire interest in a subject which is (**6**) ..... to everyday life. The Earth Galleries turn the traditional idea of the geological museum (**7**) ....., literally because you begin at the top. The central space in the museum is a glass-topped atrium. As you enter, you (**8**) ..... up to the top of this by escalator. On the (**9**) ....., the escalator passes through a massive revolving globe, measuring eleven metres (**10**) ..... diameter. This represents a planet, not necessarily the Earth. (**11**) ..... at the top, you work your way down through the six different exhibitions that (**12**) ..... the museum.

The individual exhibitions explain natural phenomena (**13**) ..... earthquakes and volcanoes as well as looking at the Earth's energy (**14**) ..... and where our most common building (**15**) ..... come from. These exhibitions allow everyone to appreciate the fascination of geology.

1	**A** pick	**B** know	**C** bound	**D** tend
2	**A** despite	**B** owing	**C** unless	**D** whether
3	**A** catch	**B** found	**C** discover	**D** convince
4	**A** further	**B** greater	**C** wider	**D** nearer
5	**A** ambition	**B** aim	**C** reason	**D** topic
6	**A** part	**B** relevant	**C** joined	**D** referred
7	**A** head to toe	**B** inside out	**C** back to front	**D** upside down
8	**A** drive	**B** ride	**C** run	**D** steer
9	**A** way	**B** route	**C** trip	**D** path
10	**A** on	**B** around	**C** across	**D** in
11	**A** From	**B** Once	**C** Got	**D** Yet
12	**A** bring together	**B** consist of	**C** make up	**D** show off
13	**A** not only	**B** such as	**C** so that	**D** in order
14	**A** resources	**B** talents	**C** treasures	**D** reservations
15	**A** ingredients	**B** substances	**C** contents	**D** materials

For Questions **16–30**, read the text below and think of the word which best fits each space. Use only **one** word in each space. There is an example at the beginning (**0**).

Write your answers **on the separate answer sheet**.

Example:	**0**	*was*

FADING MEMORIES

The instamatic camera (**0**) .... invented in 1963 and the mass marketing of colour film followed shortly after. Until then, almost (**16**) .... photographs had been in black and white. (**17**) .... the early 1970s, sales of colour film had overtaken those for black and white and today colour accounts (**18**) .... all but a tiny percentage of the 96 million films sold in Britain every year.

But those early colour photographs are already showing (**19**) .... of age. Millions of snapshots (**20**) .... since 1963 are changing colour because of their chemical make (**21**) .... These chemicals change over time. The deterioration of photographs is nothing new, of course. We tend (**22**) .... view the late nineteenth century in delicate shades of brown thanks to the chemicals used at the time. But (**23**) .... is a fair chance that future generations will (**24**) .... back at the late twentieth century as the era of purple grass and pink skies. Because, (**25**) .... the fading is only gradual, the different colours change (**26**) .... different rates.

Keeping photographs in a dark drawer, (**27**) .... even in the fridge, will certainly (**28**) .... them last longer, but none of (**29**) .... will keep forever. Our grandparents' old-fashioned black and white photographs from earlier in the twentieth century will (**30**) .... the test of time better, in fact.

For Questions **31–40**, complete the second sentence so that it has a similar meaning to the first sentence, using the word given. **Do not change the word given.** You must use between two and five words, including the word given. Here is an example (**0**).

Example: **0** 'A bad headache made it impossible for me to attend school,' Alan said to his teacher.

missed

Alan told his teacher that he .... a bad headache.

The gap can be filled by the words 'had missed school because of' so you write:

0	had missed school because of

Write **only the missing words** on the separate answer sheet.

---

31 I am not strong enough to climb that steep path without a walking stick.

too

That path is .... climb without a walking stick.

32 That man stole a valuable picture but he was never punished.

got

That man .... a valuable picture.

33 Hitch-hiking is less popular now than ten years ago.

not

Hitch-hiking is .... was ten years ago.

34 'Why did you cancel the party, Lucy?' Martin asked.

called

Martin asked Lucy .... the party.

35 'We shall tell your parents that you are often absent from school,' Mrs Clerk said.

would

Mrs Clerk said to me that my parents .... my frequent absences from school.

36 'Do not leave your belongings unattended,' the group leader said to the tourists.

to

The group leader told the tourists .... belongings unattended.

37 Mrs Butler didn't buy her son a bicycle because she didn't have enough money.

afford

Mrs Butler .... her son a bicycle.

38 Sally will not buy that pony because she is no longer interested.

lost

Sally .... buying that pony.

39 Although it looks easy, that dance is actually quite difficult.

not

That dance is .... looks.

40 Take your mobile phone because the car might break down.

case

Take your mobile phone .... down.

For Questions **41–55**, read the text below and look carefully at each line. Some of the lines are correct, and some have a word which should not be there.

If a line is correct, put a tick (✔) by the number **on the separate answer sheet**. If a line has a word which should not be there, write the word **on the separate answer sheet**. There are examples at the beginning (**0** and **00**).

Examples:	**0**	*or*
	00	✔

0	....	I had a wonderful experience or last weekend and I
00	....	would like to tell you about it. Once a month I spend a
41	....	weekend away with two friends. We usually prefer sleep in
42	....	our tents, but sometimes when we feel like to having
43	....	a real rest, we book a room in a hotel. On Thursday evening,
44	....	I suggested them that we should go on a 'mystery weekend'
45	....	and they agreed with at once. On Saturday morning, we got into
46	....	my father's car, one which I had borrowed for the weekend.
47	....	No-one else knew for how long the drive would be. I was
48	....	the only one who knew it where we were going. I had been
49	....	busy on the telephone that morning making all the hotel
50	....	arrangements. Where do you think I took them off?
51	....	To the Bond Marina Hotel, on the banks of the River Dart,
52	....	where a boat was got ready to take us all on a trip up
53	....	the river. It was such a lovely day that we sat on the seats
54	....	on deck and enjoyed ourselves the sunshine. When we got
55	....	home on Sunday, everyone wanted another 'mystery weekend'!

For Questions **56–65**, read the text below. Use the word given in capitals at the end of each line to form a word that fits in the space in the same line. There is an example at the beginning (**0**). Write your answers **on the separate answer sheet**.

Example:	**0**	*flightless*

Penguins are (**0**) ..*flightless*.. birds which live south of the Equator. As their **FLIGHT**
legs are short, they (**56**) .... stand upright and walk when they are **USUAL**
on land. When they find it (**57**) .... to travel at greater speed, they **NEED**
often drop on to their stomachs and slide along. But it is at sea,
(**58**) .... when diving, that penguins really move fast, the **SPECIAL**
(**59**) .... of their streamlined bodies allowing them to reach a **WEIGH**
(**60**) .... of up to 265 metres in some cases. **DEEP**

The sixteen species of penguin tend to look rather (**61**) .... **LIKE**
with black or dark blue backs and white fronts. But (**62**) .... **VARY**
in size and head patterns allow them to be (**63**) .... The **IDENTIFY**
fact that a number of species spend their whole life in Antarctica
where there is little (**64**) .... from the world's least **PROTECT**
(**65**) .... weather conditions, makes their continued survival one **WELCOME**
of the wonders of the nature.

PAPER 4   Listening (40 minutes)

You will hear people talking in eight different situations. For Questions **1–8**, choose the best answer **A**, **B** or **C**.

1   You hear a man and a woman talking about something they bought in a shop.
    What is the man going to complain about?
    A   faulty goods
    B   poor value for money
    C   lack of information about goods

    [ ] 1

2   You hear a woman talking to a friend.
    What is she talking about?
    A   travelling by public transport
    B   waiting in queues
    C   joining a social club

    [ ] 2

3   You hear a man talking about wearing hats.
    Why didn't he like wearing a hat at the wedding?
    A   It was the wrong size.
    B   People laughed at him.
    C   He felt uncomfortable in it.

    [ ] 3

4   You hear someone comparing life in the town with life in the country.
    What is his view of the country?
    A   He never wants to go there again.
    B   He can understand why people go there.
    C   He wonders what people find to do there.

    [ ] 4

5   You hear a mother talking about her young son.
    How does she feel when she watches him in class?
    A   ashamed of herself
    B   disappointed in him
    C   curious about his teacher

    [ ] 5

6   You hear an announcement on the radio.
    Why should listeners call the programme?
    A   to find out about science fiction
    B   to ask questions about an author
    C   to get ideas about how to be a writer

    [ ] 6

7   You hear the beginning of a radio programme about the food at tourist attractions.
    What point is being made about the attractions?
    A   People have little choice of food there.
    B   People like the kind of food served there.
    C   People choose the unhealthiest food there.

    [ ] 7

8   You turn on the radio in the middle of something.
    What are you listening to?
    A   travel news
    B   weather forecast
    C   cookery feature

    [ ] 8

You will hear an interview with the actor Alex Beringer. For Questions **9–18**, complete the sentences.

Alex was at the [**9**] when he was invited to be in a film.

For his first film, Alex had to get rid of his [**10**]

Alex was paid little for his first film because the [**11**] was small.

When he was younger, Alex's mother used to read [**12**] to him.

Alex's father wanted him to be a [**13**]

Alex changed his hair colour to [**14**]

Alex is now playing the role of a [**15**]

Alex says he prefers to play [**16**] characters.

Alex says that many famous stars are [**17**] people.

In the future, Alex would like to [**18**]

You will hear five students saying what makes them successful in their studies. For Questions **19–23**, choose from the list **A–F** what each speaker says. Use the letters only once. There is one extra letter which you do not need to use.

What makes you successful in your studies?

A   I can study long hours.

B   I am helped by others.

C   I pay attention.

D   I read extra materials.

E   I study only what is important.

F   I have a good memory.

Speaker 1	19
Speaker 2	20
Speaker 3	21
Speaker 4	22
Speaker 5	23

You will hear a radio interview with Dave Salter, a deep-sea diving instructor. For Questions **24–30**, choose the best answer **A**, **B** or **C**.

24   Why did Dave consider a full-time career as a diving instructor?
   A   He had always liked teaching.
   B   His trainees were pleased with him.
   C   It was a chance to earn more money.

[24]

25   David says instructors must
   A   understand weather conditions.
   B   know the best diving areas.
   C   be patient with their trainees.

[25]

26   When does Dave become nervous?
   A   When students become agressive.
   B   When his students leave the group.
   C   When other divers get close to his group.

[26]

27   What mistake did the girl called Elaine make?
   A   She did not get on well with her group.
   B   She mistook Dave for somebody else.
   C   She went off alone.

[27]

28   How did David feel after the conversation with Mr and Mrs Jones?
   A   embarrassed
   B   upset
   C   impatient

[28]

29   What does Dave find boring in his job?
   A   allowing students time for photos
   B   repeating instructions for students
   C   following the same routine

[29]

30   What would Dave like to be in the future?
   A   a photographer
   B   a secretary
   C   a manager

[30]

PAPER 5

Speaking (14 minutes)

PART 1 (3 minutes)

Answer these questions:

What is your favourite type of music?
Has your taste in music changed over the years? Why / Why not?
Where do you like to listen to music?
What effect do different types of music have on you?

PART 2 (3 or 4 minutes)

Workplaces (compare, contrast and speculate)

Turn to pictures 1 and 2 on page 172 which show people in their workplaces.

Candidate A, compare and contrast these photographs, and say how you think the people feel about the place where they work. You have a minute to do this.

Candidate B, do you like a tidy place to work or study?

Dancing (compare, contrast and speculate)

Turn to pictures 1 and 2 on page 173 which show people dancing.

Candidate B, compare and contrast these photographs, and say how you think the people feel about dancing. You have a minute to do this.

Candidate A, are you a good dancer?

PART 3 (3 or 4 minutes)

Summer courses (discuss and evaluate)

Turn to the pictures on page 174 which show different ideas for a leaflet about summer courses for young people at a British language school. Imagine you have to choose which pictures will appear in the leaflet.

How successful would each picture be in showing life at the school? Which three pictures do you think should appear in the leaflet?

PART 4 (3 or 4 minutes)

Answer these questions:

Do you think a summer course is a good way to learn a language?
What are the advantages of studying a language in the country where it is spoken?
Do you like to do things on holiday, or would you rather just relax?
How many languages do you think children should study in school?

Candidate A

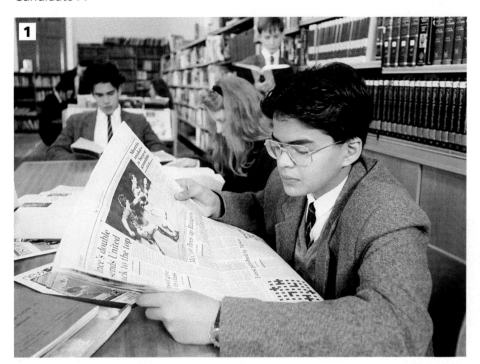

Useful phrases

Well, there are people reading newspapers *in both photos. In the first photo*, it's a boy in a library, *in the second*, a man, maybe in an office.

The boy seems to be reading the sports page. *Perhaps* he's having a rest between lessons.

I get the impression that the man is not very comfortable sitting on the table.

He looks like he's …

Candidate B

Useful phrases

The young people in these photos are showing very different feelings, the boy is not happy at all while the girl is having a very good time.

In this photo, I think the mother is telling him that he is not allowed to go out.

Perhaps he has homework to do. Or maybe he is being punished for breaking something.

I think the mother probably reads to her daughter every evening and they both look forward to it.

Candidates A and B

Useful phrases

Most young people would love to work in a television company, *don't you think*?

In my opinion, some of these jobs require training and may be very difficult for somebody without the necessary skills. *Would you agree with that?*

Yes, that's a good point.

In this job they can learn how to communicate effectively, and that's a very useful skill.

Now, in which two jobs would they learn the most useful skills? *What do you think?*

My first choice would be …

I'm not sure I agree with that. Don't you think …

Candidate A

Candidate B

Candidates A and B

Candidate A

Candidate B

Candidates A and B

Candidate A

Candidate B

Candidates A and B

Candidate A

Candidate B

Candidates A and B

Candidate A

1

2

VISUALS

Candidate B

Candidates A and B

VISUALS

Candidate A

Candidate B

Candidates A and B

Timetable

Friday	pm	_____
Saturday	am	_____
Saturday	pm	_____
Sunday	am	_____
Sunday	pm	_____

Candidate A

Candidate B

Candidates A and B

SAMPLE

UNIVERSITY of CAMBRIDGE
Local Examinations Syndicate

Centre No.

Candidate Name
If not already printed, write name
in CAPITALS and complete the
Candidate No. grid (in pencil).
Candidate's signature

Candidate No.

Examination Title

Examination
Details

Centre

Supervisor:
☒ If the candidate is ABSENT or has WITHDRAWN shade here ▭

Candidate Answer Sheet: FCE paper 3 Use of English

Use a pencil

For **Part 1**: Mark ONE letter for each question.

For example, if you think **C** is the
right answer to the question,
mark your answer sheet like this:

| 0 | A | B | C | D |

For **Parts 2, 3, 4 and 5**: Write your
answers in the spaces next to the
numbers like this:

| 0 | |

Part 1

	A	B	C	D
1	A	B	C	D
2	A	B	C	D
3	A	B	C	D
4	A	B	C	D
5	A	B	C	D
6	A	B	C	D
7	A	B	C	D
8	A	B	C	D
9	A	B	C	D
10	A	B	C	D
11	A	B	C	D
12	A	B	C	D
13	A	B	C	D
14	A	B	C	D
15	A	B	C	D

Part 2

		Do not write here
16		16
17		17
18		18
19		19
20		20
21		21
22		22
23		23
24		24
25		25
26		26
27		27
28		28
29		29
30		30

Turn
over
for
Parts
3 - 5 ↑

DP319/93

FCE-3

Part 3

		Do not write here
31		31 0 1 2
32		32 0 1 2
33		33 0 1 2
34		34 0 1 2
35		35 0 1 2
36		36 0 1 2
37		37 0 1 2
38		38 0 1 2
39		39 0 1 2
40		40 0 1 2

Part 4

		Do not write here
41		41
42		42
43		43
44		44
45		45
46		46
47		47
48		48
49		49
50		50
51		51
52		52
53		53
54		54
55		55

Part 5

		Do not write here
56		56
57		57
58		58
59		59
60		60
61		61
62		62
63		63
64		64
65		65